T0372341

Why are Presidential Regimes Bad for the Economy?

Recent evidence suggests that macroeconomic outcomes are inferior in countries operating under presidential regimes compared with those with parliaments, with lower levels of economic growth, higher rates of inflation, and higher levels of income inequality in countries with presidential governments. Despite this, more heads of state look to consolidate and build their executive power. This book considers why presidential regimes, in particular, are so bad for the economy.

Throughout the book, the authors comprehensively and simultaneously consider the impact of legal, political, and economic institutions on the mechanisms. It is first demonstrated that presidential countries have (on average) inferior outcomes relative to parliamentary states with respect to these institutions and, moreover, with respect to healthcare and human development indicators. Subsequently, the book explores the impact of constitutional choice (parliamentary versus presidential) on both institutions and macroeconomic outcomes. It is documented that having a presidential regime induces weaker institutions, but that quality institutions can mitigate some of the negative impacts of such regimes.

Dr Richard McManus is Director of Research Development at Christ Church Business School and is Reader in Macroeconomic Policy. His main research interests are in the area of the impact of government on macroeconomic outcomes.

Gulcin Ozkan is Professor of Finance at King's College, London. Her research focuses on the intersection of macroeconomics and finance covering issues such as financial crises, financial stability, monetary and macroprudential policies, emerging markets, public debt, fiscal policy, and financial constraints, and the economics of constitutions.

Routledge Frontiers of Political Economy

Money and Capital
A Critique of Monetary Thought, the Dollar and Post-Capitalism
Laurent Baronian

Modern Money and the Rise and Fall of Capitalist Finance
The Institutionalization of Trusts, Personae, and Indebtedness
Jongchul Kim

Innovation, Complexity and Economic Evolution
From Theory to Policy
Pier Paolo Saviotti

Economic Growth and Inequality
The Economist's Dilemma
Laurent Dobuzinskis

Wellbeing, Nature and Moral Values in Economics
How Modern Economic Analysis Faces the Challenges Ahead
Heinz Welsch

Why are Presidential Regimes Bad for the Economy?
Understanding the Link Between Forms of Government and
Economic Outcomes
Richard McManus and Gulcin Ozkan

Critical Theory and Economics
Philosophical Notes on Contemporary Inequality
Robin Maialeh

For more information about this series, please visit: www.routledge.com/
Routledge-Frontiers-of-Political-Economy/book-series/SE0345

Why are Presidential Regimes Bad for the Economy?

Understanding the Link Between Forms of Government and Economic Outcomes

**Richard McManus and
Gulcin Ozkan**

Routledge
Taylor & Francis Group

LONDON AND NEW YORK

First published 2023
by Routledge
4 Park Square, Milton Park, Abingdon, Oxon OX14 4RN

and by Routledge
605 Third Avenue, New York, NY 10158

Routledge is an imprint of the Taylor & Francis Group, an informa business

British Library Cataloguing-in-Publication Data
A catalogue record for this book is available from the British Library

ISBN: 978-0-367-69286-5 (hbk)
ISBN: 978-0-367-69287-2 (pbk)
ISBN: 978-1-003-14124-2 (ebk)

DOI: 10.4324/9781003141242

Typeset in Times New Roman
by Apex CoVantage, LLC

To the memory of our mothers.

Contents

1 Introduction and overview

How countries are run and what impact this has on constituents are existential questions that preoccupied philosophers, political scientists, and politicians at least since the 19th century. A key aspect of governance is related to how the executive, legislative, and judiciary are organised and structured. The separation of power and hierarchy among the three functions is, in turn, closely linked to the form of government, ranging from parliamentary democracies to presidential systems, including regimes that combine components of both as intermediate arrangements.

While constitutions underlying the forms of government tend to change little over time, constitutional reforms usually come in clusters. For example, a large number of changes in constitutional rules were enacted in the immediate aftermath of both the First and Second World Wars (see, for example, Price 1943; Scarrow 1974). Similarly, the early 1990s witnessed an intense debate on governance systems for two obvious reasons. First, the proliferation of independent nations in Eastern Europe following the collapse of the Soviet Union revived the debate on 'optimal system of government'.[1] Second, and concurrently, several countries in Latin America were emerging from a series of government failures, military coups, and economic collapse, forcing a serious assessment of the region's system of government – mostly presidential regimes – relative to the alternative of parliamentarism (see, for example, Carey 2014).

More recently, constitutional reform has received much attention in several countries in the Middle East with the outbreak of the 'Arab Spring' in 2013, which reignited the debate on government systems. For example, whether Egypt should move from its presidential regime into an alternative parliamentary one was widely discussed. Turkey, on the other hand, made the move in the opposite direction where a referendum in April 2017 paved the way for the country to abandon its parliamentary regime in favour of an 'executive presidential' system bestowing excessive powers on the president (see, for example, Kirişçi and Toygür 2019 and Somer 2019).

DOI: 10.4324/9781003141242-1

Similarly, Kyrgyzstan where a parliamentary system was adopted in 2010 switched to a presidential regime in May 2021 (Engvall 2022).

1.1 Parliamentarism versus presidentialism

Comparative analyses of presidential versus parliamentary systems go as far back as the second half of the 19th century. In their leading analyses of the advantages and disadvantages of the two regimes, both Walter Bagehot and Woodrow Wilson argued for the primacy of parliamentary systems over presidential regimes. This was on account of the executive being always responsible to the elected assembly and hence to the electorate in parliamentary systems. The cabinet (the 'executive') still possesses sufficient control in parliamentary regimes to form appropriate national policy, given it retains the power to dissolve the parliament if its proposed laws are not enacted. Woodrow Wilson found such a system more favourable than the US' presidential one with endless disputes between the executive and the Congress (Price 1943).

Juan Linz led the debate on the comparative assessment of presidential versus parliamentary systems as an increasing number of countries were transitioning to democracy in the early 1990s. Linz (1990) argued that presidential regimes – where the president is the chief executive and is elected by popular vote – are less conducive to stable democracy than parliamentary regimes, pointing to the 'perils of presidentialism'. A substantial body of subsequent work has reiterated that democratic consolidation is stronger under parliamentarism relative to that under presidentialism, leading to greater democratic stability under the former relative to the latter (Mainwaring 1990, Shugart and Carey 1992, Linz 1994, Stepan and Skach 1993, and Cheibub *et al.* 2004).

It is widely observed that the only presidential system that has exhibited constitutional continuity has been that of the United States of America (see, for example, Riggs 1988). France and Finland, the other two regimes featuring some elements of presidential systems that are also stable democracies, are both mixed arrangements also displaying elements of parliamentary systems (see, for example, Cheibub *et al.* 2010).

South American presidential regimes have also provided plenty of evidence for presidentialism being less durable than parliamentarism (see, for example, Hochstetler and Edwards 2009). Although parliamentary democracies too have exhibited instability, political crises are often resolved without turning into regime crises under parliamentary systems. To put it differently, while parliamentary regimes may also exhibit *government instability,* presidential systems are prone to *regime instability* (Tsebelis 1995). Moreover, parliamentary democracies are seen as better at crisis resolution even in highly polarised, divided societies (Linz 1994, Lijphart 2004 and 2012, Murphy 2020); India is often mentioned as a case in point. More recently, parliaments have been hailed as the best mechanisms for coordinating effective responses in the face of major crises, as evidenced during the COVID-19 episode in 2020 (see, for example, Murphy 2020).

Is this a coincidence or an outcome of the functioning of the two systems? Why do presidential regimes create instability? Existing work points to the following by-products of presidential regimes as sources of instability: (1) the clear distinction between the winners and losers in presidential elections and the fact that the gains and the losses are defined for the entire presidential term; (2) the competing claims to legitimacy of both the president and the assembly leading to divided government with serious implications for the stability of democratic systems; (3) the rigidity created by the fixed presidential term; and (4) the too-powerful nature of the presidential office (Linz 1990, Riggs 1993, Stepan and Skach 1993).

Others pointed to the advantages of presidential regimes that may counterbalance some of their handicaps. For example, it is argued that presidential systems offer greater choice to the electorate who can vote for both the chief executive and the legislative assembly. In addition, it is suggested that there is a more direct link between the choices made at the ballot box and the electoral outcomes under presidentialism, in contrast to parliamentary systems in which coalition formations may weaken this link, reducing the accountability under the latter (see, for example, Mainwaring and Shugart 1997). Moreover, it is contended that it was not the presidentialism *per se* but the power of the executive in these regimes that led to democratic instability (Shugart and Carey 1992).[2] It is also asserted that the decisiveness of the executive and hence a strong president can be beneficial in unifying political factions, expanding the core political centre, and encouraging dialogue (see, for example, Ellis and Samuel 2009).

1.2 Economic effects of government systems

While the consequences of constitutional rules including the form of government have been a subject of investigation since at least the late 19th century, work on the implications of this choice for economic outcomes only started to emerge in the early 2000s. Indeed, the burgeoning research on political economy throughout the 1990s uncovering the effects of both economic and political institutions prepared the ground for a formal examination of how constitutional rules impact the economy (see, for example, Scully 1988, Shleifer and Vishny 1994, Mauro 1995, Barro 1998, 2007, Rodrik 2000, and Acemoglu *et al.* 2001).

In their seminal work, Persson and Tabellini (2003; henceforth 'PT2003') establish a number of links between constitutions and economic outcomes, particularly regarding government size and public finances. This follows from Persson *et al.* (2000)'s prediction of larger governments (higher taxes and overall spending) in parliamentary systems, which in turn, arises from the differences in the functioning of the two systems of government. For example, the vote of confidence required in parliamentary regimes creates incentives for strong party discipline encouraging spending towards broad programmes in pursuit of voters' interests, resulting in higher spending and higher taxes. PT2003 provide supporting evidence for this hypothesis where both public and welfare spending as a proportion of national income is shown to be significantly lower under presidential regimes, as compared with those under parliamentary systems, particularly in old and advanced democracies.

A central question related to the role the form of government plays in the economy is whether it is possible to rank government systems in terms of economic performance. This question is taken up in our earlier work which has established that macroeconomic outcomes are inferior in countries operating under presidential regimes compared with those under parliamentary systems. Using data on per capita income growth, inflation, and income inequality as key measures of economic performance, McManus and Ozkan (2018; henceforth 'MO2018') found that annual output growth is between 0.6 and 1.2 percentage points lower and inflation is 4 percentage points higher under presidential regimes relative to those under parliamentary ones. Further, our findings revealed that income inequality is between 12 and 24 percentage points greater under presidential systems relative to those under parliamentary regimes.

In a separate line of inquiry, Gerring *et al.* (2009) established that presidential regimes also led to worse political, economic, and human development outcomes. They find that parliamentary systems have created more favourable conditions for education, investment, and external trade, resulting in higher per capita income as well as improved life expectancy.

As is widely acknowledged, disentangling the role of constitutional rules on outcomes is inherently difficult given the list of factors that are likely to influence both such rules and outcomes arising from those rules. Attempts at remedying such reverse causality have been a core focus in much of the existing work investigating economic consequences of constitutions (see, for example, Blume *et al.* 2009, Gregorini and Longoni 2009, Knutsen 2011, Rockey 2012 and MO2018).

While there has been significant progress in uncovering the economic effects of constitutions since the publication of PT2003's seminal work nearly 20 years ago, we still have little understanding of the mechanisms through which government systems shape economic outcomes. It is therefore still unclear why presidential regimes consistently do worse than parliamentary ones on the economy. This is the main motivation underlying our work in this book in which we aim to present a systematic cross-country analysis of the channels through which form of government influences economic performance. By doing so, we attempt to answer questions such as 'What drives the difference in macroeconomic outcomes between parliamentary and presidential regimes? Are these outcomes an innate component of government systems, or are there certain compounded factors that are more prevalent in one regime compared to the other? What are the quantitative impacts of such factors on economic outcomes?'

Our conjecture here is that constitutional rules shape economic outcomes through their role in the form of institutions and, in turn, through the influence of institutions on economic policy and thereby on economic outcomes.

1.3 Regime choice, institutions, and economic outcomes

It has long been recognised that institutions, whether political, legal, or economic, play a key role in economic outcomes by aggregating conflicting interests into public policy and imposing constraints on economic behaviour (see, for example, North 1990 and 1993, Eichengreen and Iversen 1999, Hall and Jones 1999, Nickell and Layard 1999, Rodrik 2004, and Granovetter 2005). The proliferation of work on institutional economics over the recent decades has led to significant progress in identifying the role of institutions in the proper functioning of economies and consequently in economic outcomes (Rodrik *et al.* 2004, Acemoglu and Robinson 2008, Acemoglu and Johnson 2005, North 2005a, 2005b). It is now widely recognized that good institutions accompany good economic governance, leading to superior economic outcomes, underlying our motivation in focussing on institutions as key channels through which constitutions impact economic outcomes.

Our hypothesis in this book is that this link works through the constitutional form's impact on political, legal, and economic institutions. We propose that government systems impact economic outcomes by influencing and interacting with institutions. It therefore follows that the economic effects of presidential regimes will differ from those of parliamentary ones to the extent that the institutions under the former differ from those under the latter. Both PT2003 and Gerring *et al.* (2009) also pointed to the importance of institutions and quality of governance as important factors in determining the wider consequences of constitutional form.

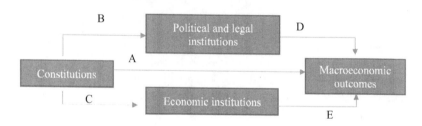

Figure 1.1 A schematic view of linkages between constitutions, institutions, and economic outcomes

Following these arguments, we propose that interactions between the constitutional form, institutions, and economic outcomes can be formalised as in Figure 1.1.

As stated earlier, existing work has established the role of government form in macroeconomic outcomes such as public spending, per capita income, inflation, economic growth, and income inequality (PT2003, Knutsen 2009, Rockey 2012, MO2018). This *direct* link between constitutions and economic outcomes is represented by arrow A in Figure 1.1. In this book, we explore *how* constitutions impact economic outcomes *through their role in the choice of institutions*, arrows B and C, and *how those institutions influence economic outcomes*, as displayed by D and E, in addition to the direct link between the two as indicated by arrow A.

There is another reason why we choose to focus on the role of institutions as the main channels through which government systems impact outcomes and hence as a central determinant of economic performance. This is related to an important common trend in governance over the last two decades in the form of an unmistakable retreat in democracy, that intensified in the aftermath of the global financial crisis in 2008–2009. Despite the great expectations about the future of global democracy in the early 1990s following the emergence of a cluster of independent nations in Europe, the move towards greater democracy subsequently stalled and reversed. For example, *the Democracy Index* of the Economist's Intelligence Unit produced the worst global score in 2021 since their records began in 2006, revealing that only 45.7% of the global population now live in 'a democracy of some sort'. Moreover, it is reported that only 6.4% of the world population are now habitants of countries classified as 'full democracies'.[3]

At the same time, there has been a clear drift towards populism and the rise of autocratic regimes, also documented by the *Variety of Democracy*, 2022 report, establishing that 'the level of democracy enjoyed by the global citizen in 2021 is down to 1989 levels'.[4] Interestingly, this intensification in the deterioration of democracy is not confined to the less developed parts of the world. The United States, for example, was downgraded to the 'flawed democracy' group from the 'full democracy' one in 2016.

The expansion in authoritarian rule has also been visible in measures of freedom, provided by the Freedom House. *The Freedom of the World Index* 2021 displays 16 consecutive years of decline in measured freedoms across the globe. The number of countries whose freedom score fell outnumbered those whose score improved every year since 2006, establishing that only about 20% of the world population now live in 'free countries'.

Such backsliding in democracy has entailed deterioration in multiple spheres. The retreat in freedoms and democracy has taken drastic forms in some cases such as the military taking control in Sudan and Burma. Meanwhile, freely elected governments in countries such as Brazil, Hungary, India, Turkey, and Poland presided over a series of antidemocratic actions including infringement of the rule of law and violations of freedom of speech and media capture (Freedom House 2022). Even well-established democracies such as the United States have been subject to illiberal forces, culminating in the violent storming of the Capitol Hall in an attempt to prevent the affirmation of the 2020 presidential elections. In our view, this widespread deterioration in democratic institutions and the rise of authoritarian regimes across the globe underscore the need for a systematic analysis of how democratic institutions interact with government systems in shaping economic outcomes.

1.4 Road map

In what follows, we will first revisit the economic effects of government systems by providing additional data and analysis in Chapter 2 which focuses, albeit informally, on the *direct* effect of the government type on economic outcomes. We then explore channels through which government systems can influence economic outcomes, by carefully examining the role of both economic and political institutions, establishing a clear mapping between the former and the latter. More specifically, Chapter 3 examines whether there are economically and statistically meaningful differences in institutions under the presidential versus parliamentary regimes. Chapter 4 then combines both the *direct* and *indirect* effects of government systems in formal estimation where the latter is postulated to work through the government systems' influence in shaping institutions. In so doing, Chapter 4 investigates whether there is empirical support for alternative channels, by first studying whether and how these channels differ under different government systems and then if they are linked to macroeconomic outcomes.

Chapter 4 also presents a battery of tests to identify the direction of causality between the economic outcomes and institutional variables. Chapter 5 presents a discussion of the empirical findings in earlier chapters and offers some concluding remarks.

This book is written for a number of different audiences. Given the general interest in the issues taken up in our analysis, we have tried to make our arguments in a relatively non-technical way, with the exception of Chapter 4. Readers who are unfamiliar with formal techniques used in economics can skip Chapter 4 and can still get the gist of our arguments and ideas from Chapters 1, 2, 3, and 5. The material we present throughout the book should be accessible to most final-year undergraduate and or first-year graduate students of economics and/or politics.

Notes

1 The quest for the appropriate form of government lasted much longer for some countries in Eastern Europe. For example, both Croatia and Moldova moved to parliamentary systems – their current regimes – in 2000 (see, for example, Fish and Kroenig 2009 and Roper 2008).
2 Morgenstern *et al.* (2020) dispute this result by using a new methodology in measuring presidential power.
3 See p. 6, *The Democracy Index*, 2021, The Economist Intelligence Unit, 2022.
4 See p. 6, *The Variety of Democracy* 2022 report.

References

Acemoglu, D. and Johnson, S. (2005) 'Unbundling institutions', *Journal of Political Economy*, 113(5), 949–995.

Acemoglu, D., Johnson, S. and Robinson, J.A. (2001) 'The colonial origins of comparative development: An empirical investigation', *American Economic Review*, 91(5), 1369–1401.

Acemoglu, D. and Robinson, J. (2008) *The Role of Institutions in Growth and Development*. Vol. 10. Washington, DC: World Bank.

Barro, R. (1998) *Determinants of Economic Growth: A Cross-Country Empirical Study*. Edition 1, Vol. 1. Cambridge, MA and London: MIT Press Books, The MIT Press.

Barro, R. (2007) 'Democracy and growth', *Journal of Economic Growth*, 1(1)(1996), 1–27.

Blume, L., Müller, J., Voigt, S. and Wolf, C. (2009) 'The economic effects of constitutions: Replicating – and extending – Persson and Tabellini', *Public Choice*, 139(1–2), 197–225.

Carey, J.M. (2014) 'Presidentialism 25 years after Linz', Keynote address at the Conference on Coalitional Presidentialism at St. Anthony's College, Oxford, on May 2, 2014.

Cheibub, J.A., Gandhi, J. and Vreeland, J.R. (2010) 'Democracy and dictatorship revisited', *Public Choice*, 143(1–2), 67–101.

Cheibub, J.A., Przeworski, A. and Saiegh, S.M. (2004) 'Government coalitions and legislative success under presidentialism and parliamentarism', *British Journal of Political Science*, 34(4), 565–587.

Eichengreen, B. and Iversen, T. (1999) 'Institutions and economic performance: Evidence from the labour market', *Oxford Review of Economic Policy*, 15(4), 121–138.

Ellis, A. and Samuels, K. (2009) *Making presidentialism work: Sharing and learning from global experience*. Cómo Hacer Que Funcione el Sistema Presidencial (Making presidentialism work). México, DF: Universidad Nacional Autónoma de México-Instituto de Investigaciones Jurídicas.

Engvall, J. (2022) 'Between bandits and bureaucrats: 30 years of parliamentary development in Kyrgyzstan', Central Asia-Caucasus Institute & Silk Road Studies Program Silk Road Paper, available at www.silkroadstudies.org/publications/silkroad-papers-and-monographs/item/13434-between-bandits-and-bureaucrats-30-years-of-parliamentary-development-in-kyrgyzstan.html

Fish, M.S. and Kroenig, M. (2009) *The Handbook of National Legislatures: A Global Survey*. Cambridge: Cambridge University Press.

Freedom House (2022) Freedom in the World 2022. https://freedomhouse.org/sites/default/files/2022-02/FIW_2022_PDF_Booklet_Digital_Final_Web.pdf

Gerring, J., Thacker, S.C. and Moreno, C. (2009) 'Are parliamentary systems better?', *Comparative Political Studies*, 42(3), 327–359.

Granovetter, M. (2005) 'The impact of social structure on economic outcomes', *Journal of Economic Perspectives*, 19(1), 33–50.

Gregorini, F. and Longoni, E. (2009) 'Inequality, political systems and public spending', Technical report.

Hall, R.E. and Jones, C.I. (1999) 'Why do some countries produce so much more output per worker than others?', *The Quarterly Journal of Economics*, 114(1), 83–116.

Hochstetler, K. and Edwards, M.E. (2009) 'Failed presidencies: Identifying and explaining a South American anomaly', *Journal of Politics in Latin America*, 1(2), 31–57.

Kirişçi, K. and Toygür, I. (2019) 'Turkey's new presidential system and a changing West: Implications for Turkish foreign policy and Turkey-West relations', Turkey Project Policy Paper, 15.

Knutsen, C.H. (2009) 'The economic growth effect of constitutions revisited', Technical report, Department of Political Science, University of Oslo.

Knutsen, C.H. (2011) 'Which democracies prosper? Electoral rules, form of government and economic growth', *Electoral Studies*, 30(1), 83–90.

Lijphart, A. (2004) 'Constitutional design for divided societies', *Journal of Democracy*, 15(2), 96–109.

Lijphart, A. (2012) *Patterns of Democracy: Government Forms and Performance in Thirty-six Countries*. New Haven: Yale University Press.

Linz, J. (1990) 'The perils of presidentialism', *Journal of Democracy*, 1(1), 51–69.

Linz, J. (1994) 'Presidential or parliamentary democracy: Does it make a difference?', in J.J. Linz and A. Valenzuela (eds.), *The Failure of Presidential Democracy*. Baltimore: John Hopkins University Press, pp. 3–87.

Mainwaring, S. (1990) 'Presidentialism in Latin America', *Latin American Research Review*, 25(1), 157–179.

Mainwaring, S. and Shugart, M.S. (1997) 'Juan Linz, Presidentialism, and democracy: A critical appraisal', *Comparative Politics*, 29(4), 449–471.

Mauro, P. (1995) 'Corruption and growth', *The Quarterly Journal of Economics*, 110(3), 681–712.

McManus, R. and Ozkan, F.G. (2018) 'Who does better for the economy? Presidents versus parliamentary democracies', *Public Choice*, 176, 361–387.

Morgenstern, S., Perez, A. and Peterson, M. (2020) 'Revisiting Shugart and Carey's relation of executive powers and democratic breakdown', *Political Studies Review*, 18(1), 125–144.

Murphy, J. (2020) 'Parliaments and crises: Challenges and innovation', Parliamentary Primer 1, International Institute for Democracy and Electoral Assistance, Stockholm, 2020.

Nickell, S. and Layard, R. (1999) 'Labor market institutions and economic performance', *Handbook of Labor Economics*, 3, 3029–3084.

North, D.C. (1990) *Institutions, Institutional Change and Economic Performance*. Cambridge: Cambridge University Press.

North, D.C. (1993) 'Institutions and economic performance', *Rationality, Institutions and Economic Methodology*, 2, 242–261.

North, D.C. (2005a) *Understanding the Process of Economic Change*. Princeton: Princeton University Press.

North, D.C. (2005b) 'Institutions and the performance of economics over time', in C. Ménard and M.M. Shirley (eds)., *Handbook of New Institutional Economics*. Dordrecht: Springer, pp. 21–30.

Persson, T., Roland, G. and Tabellini, G. (2000) 'Comparative politics and public finance', *Journal of Political Economy*, 108(6), 1121–1161.

Persson, T. and Tabellini, G. (2003) *The Economic Effects of Constitutions*. Cambridge, MA: The MIT Press.

Price, D.K. (1943) 'The parliamentary and presidential systems', *Public Administration Review*, 3(4), 317–334.

Riggs, F.W. (1988) 'The survival of presidentialism in America: Para-constitutional practices', *International Political Science Review*, 9(4), 247–278.

Rockey, J. (2012) 'Reconsidering the fiscal effects of constitutions', *European Journal of Political Economy*, 28(3), 313–323.

Rodrik, D. (2000) 'Institutions for high-quality growth: What they are and how to acquire them', *Studies in Comparative International Development*, 35(3), 3–31.

Rodrik, D. (2004) 'Institutions and economic performance-getting institutions right', *CESIfo DICE Report*, 2(2), 10–15.

Rodrik, D., Subramanian, A. and Trebbi, F. (2004) 'Institutions rule: The primacy of institutions over geography and integration in economic development', *Journal of Economic Growth*, 9(2), 131–165.

Roper, S.D. (2008) 'From semi-presidentialism to parliamentarism: Regime change and presidential power in Moldova', *Europe-Asia Studies*, 60(1), 113–126.

Scarrow, H.A. (1974) 'Parliamentary and presidential government compared', *Current History*, 66(394), 264–267.

Scully, G.W. (1988) 'The institutional framework and economic development', *Journal of Political Economy*, 96(3), 652–662.

Shleifer, A. and Vishny, R.W. (1994) 'Politicians and firms', *The Quarterly Journal of Economics*, 109(4), 995–1025.

Shugart, M.S. and Carey, J. (1992) *Presidents and Assemblies: Constitutional Design and Electoral Dynamics*. Cambridge: Cambridge University Press.

Somer, M. (2019) 'Turkey: The slippery slope from reformist to revolutionary polarization and democratic breakdown', *The ANNALS of the American Academy of Political and Social Science*, 681(1), 42–61.

Stepan, A. and Skach, C. (1993) 'Constitutional frameworks and democratic consolidation: Parliamentarianism versus presidentialism', *World Politics*, 46(1), 1–22.

Tsebelis, G. (1995) 'Decision making in political systems: Veto players in presidentialism, parliamentarism, multicameralism and multipartyism', *British Journal of Political Science*, 25(3), 289–325.

2 Constitutions, form of government, and macroeconomic outcomes

2.1 Introduction

As set out in Chapter 1, the core focus of this book is how and through which mechanisms government systems influence economic outcomes. In this chapter, we provide a precursor to our subsequent analyses of the channels through which the form of government impacts economic performance. We do this by revisiting the relationship between the former (form of government) and the latter (economic performance). The work in this chapter will focus on the effects of constitutions on *final outcomes*, leaving aside the mechanism through which the two are linked, which we will return to in the remaining chapters. Within these final outcomes, we also include health outcomes to consider how these differ by form of government.

An essential first step in exploring the differential effects of government systems is to establish how to classify different forms of government. Existing classifications across government systems are commonly made on the basis of two important aspects of governance. First is the separation of power within the legislative assembly underlying the hierarchy between the executive and the legislative branches. Systems where the government – executive – is not responsible to the legislative arm and as such cannot be removed from office by this elected assembly are categorised as *presidential*. In contrast, a *parliamentary* government is subject to a vote of confidence in the assembly.[1] Second, countries where the head of state is popularly elected for a fixed term are classed as presidential regimes. There are also regimes combining the elements of both where a popularly elected president with a fixed term can be removed by the assembly, classified as 'semi-presidential' (see, for example, Cheibub *et al.* 2010).[2]

PT2003 similarly argue that the distinction in the form of government should be seen across two different perspectives. The first is the separation of powers within the legislative process which determines who

DOI: 10.4324/9781003141242-2

is accountable to whom in the structure of government; the second is the confidence vote classification whereby the elected assembly can remove the executive. In their empirical work, PT2003 adopt the latter and not the former for the regime classification given the relative ambiguity of the former and the clarity of the latter. Where both the president and the elected assembly have control to remove or appoint the executive, the classification of the form of government is made according to where primary control sits across these different political institutions.

For our work in this book, we utilise two sets of regime classification first from Bormann and Golder (2013: henceforth 'BG2013') and second from PT2003.[3] The BG2013 dataset contains information on regime type for 127 countries and the PT2003 dataset 85 countries, with additional 11 in the PT2003 dataset that are not in the BG2013 dataset resulting in 138 countries in total. Figure 2.1 presents the world map marked by our classification of regimes into presidential (black in Figure 2.1), semi-presidential (dark grey), and parliamentary (light grey); the list of countries with the regime classification, as displayed in Figure 2.1, is presented in Table A2.1 in the Data Appendix.

The distribution of the governance systems across the globe as displayed in Figure 2.1 suggests that while there are a greater number of countries operating under a parliamentary regime, presidential ones cover a greater land mass due to both the United States and Russia – two of the largest countries by area – being presidential countries. Also importantly, while some regions only feature one form of government such as the South American presidential regimes, both government types are in operation in all parts of the world. Moreover, the impact of including 'semi-presidential' regimes through the BG2013 definition is mainly limited to Europe and Africa.

2.2 Forms of government and the economy

As set out earlier, the debate on whether presidentialism is superior to parliamentary systems shifted focus towards the economic effects of the two regimes from the early 2000s. Existing work has established the effects of government systems on two sets of outcomes: (*i*) on economic performance and (*ii*) on political, economic, and human development indicators.

On macroeconomic performance

As is discussed in Chapter 1, our previous work in MO2018 has explored the impact of government systems on macroeconomic performance and has established that there are clear differences in economic outcomes under the presidential versus parliamentary systems, and these differences are

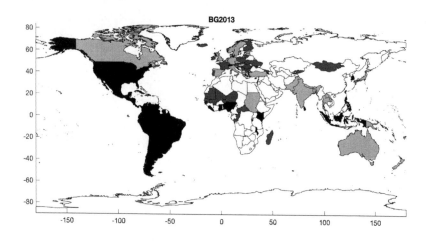

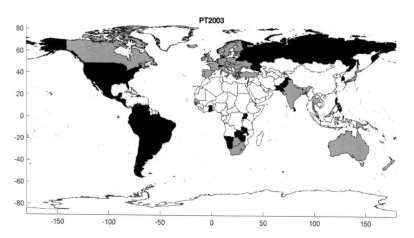

Figure 2.1 Country regime by BG2013 and PT2003.

statistically and economically significant. More specifically, MO2018 has found that presidential countries feature higher inflation, lower per capita income, and higher income inequality than their parliamentary counterparts. In this section, we revisit the effects of government type on economic performance, by examining the same set of outcomes – economic growth, inflation, and income inequality – under the two constitutional regimes over the sample period covered by the dataset we utilize in our work in this book.

Income

We start with the link between the form of government and national income. To illustrate this relationship, panel (a) of Figure 2.2 presents real GDP per capita between 1960 and 2019 for both parliamentary and presidential countries in our sample. In 1960, the median real GDP per capita was $6,260 and $1,428 in parliamentary and presidential countries, respectively (measured in 2010 US dollars). That is, for every $1 earned in a presidential country, $4.39 was earned in a parliamentary one.

Throughout the sample period, the gap between median incomes in both groups of countries has widened, consistent with the estimated lower growth rates in presidential regimes in MO2018. In 2019, the median GDP per capita was $24,659 and $5,204 in parliamentary and presidential countries (also measured in 2010 US dollars), respectively. Again, for every $1 earned in a presidential country, $4.74 was earned in a parliamentary one, pointing to the widening gap between incomes between parliamentary and presidential countries over the period.[4] Consistent through this analysis is a ***parliamentary premium*** (the ratio of GDP per capita in parliamentary countries to those of presidential ones) of between $1.5 and $7.5; that is, for every $1 earned in a presidential country, between $1.5 and $7.5 dollars are earned in parliamentary countries, depending on the date for the calculation.

Panel (b) of Figure 2.2 replicates the median path from panel (a) and now also includes the 25th and 75th percentiles (in dotted lines of the same colour) of real GDP per capita for parliamentary and presidential countries. It is observed that those countries in the bottom quartile of both cohorts have similar levels of GDP per capita. That is, lower-income countries have similar levels of income independent of the form of government. The part of the distribution that separates parliamentary and presidential countries is the top half of the income distribution. That is, conditional on a country being in the top 50% or 25% of income earners, parliamentary countries are considerably richer than presidential ones. For example, real GDP per capita in 2019 for the 75th percentile of parliamentary and presidential countries was $49,686 and $10,157, respectively, corresponding to a parliamentary premium of $4.89.

Inflation

The second key outcome considered in MO2018 is inflation – the increase in the level of prices – a central macroeconomic performance indicator. The widespread adoption of inflation targeting since the early 1990s has made inflation a core focus of the macroeconomic policy framework (see, for example, Bernanke *et al.* 1999, Mishkin 2001, King 2005, and Svensson 2010). Targeting low and steady rates of inflation has now become the norm

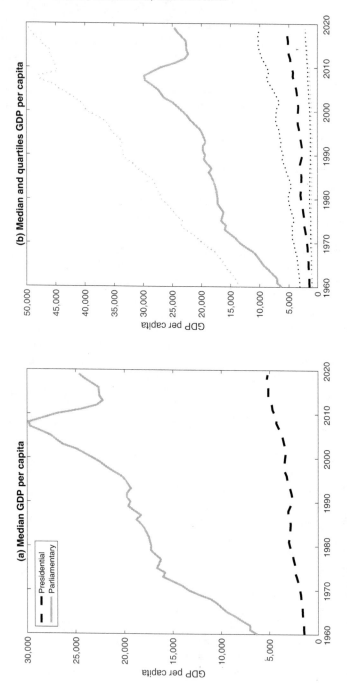

Figure 2.2 Real GDP per capita and the form of government.

across both high- and low-income countries (see, for example, Ha *et al.* 2019).

Panel (a) in Figure 2.3 presents the median consumer price index (CPI) inflation rates for both parliamentary and presidential regimes since 1960. It is apparent that the path of inflation has been similar across both sets of countries, representing the role of global factors as key drivers of inflation dynamics (see, for example, Ciccarelli and Mojon 2010, Mumtaz and Surico 2012, Carney 2015, and Kamber and Wong 2020). Nonetheless, it is also clear that presidential systems are associated with typically higher rates of average inflation than parliamentary ones, and further, there is more of a variation in inflation in the former, especially in periods of high inflation. This suggests that in times of economic stress, presidential countries struggle to keep inflation down, likely to be associated with the inferior quality of policy-making compared to parliamentary countries – an issue that will be examined in detail in Chapter 3.

Panel (b) of Figure 2.3 is similar to that of Figure 2.2 where now the first and third quartiles (in dotted lines of the same colour) for CPI inflation for parliamentary and presidential cohorts are displayed, representing the 25th and 75th percentile. There is limited evidence of a systematic trend in this panel, suggesting that the difference in inflation performance between the two cohorts is consistent across the whole distribution of inflation. Presidential regimes have both higher and more volatile rates of inflation compared to their parliamentary counterparts.[5]

Inequality

Income inequality is widely seen as a key measure with significant social, political, and economic consequences (see, for example, Easterly and Rebelo 1993, Alesina and Perotti 1996, Panizza 2002, Piketty 2003, and Piketty and Saez 2003). For example, increasing income inequality is viewed as detrimental to social cohesion and is associated with conflict, polarization, and unrest (see, for example, Shugart 1999, Bardhan 2005, and Milanovic 2018). High income inequality is also linked to unfavourable economic outcomes by (*i*) worsening health and educational outcomes, and hence human capital (Galor and Moav 2004, Stiglitz 2012); (*ii*) raising the likelihood of financial crises via over-borrowing (Rajan 2010, Bordo and Meissner 2012 and Van Treeck 2014); and (*iii*) lowering public goods provision and less effective poverty reduction (Claessens and Perotti 2007).

Figure 2.4 is similar to that of Figure 2.3, now presenting the path of pre-tax income Gini coefficients across presidential and parliamentary regimes between 1960 and 2019. Gini coefficients measure inequality

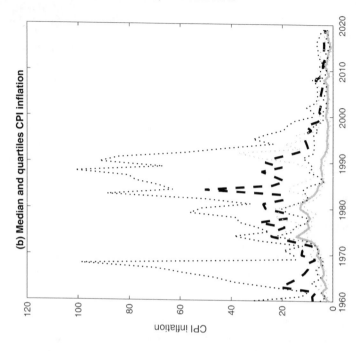

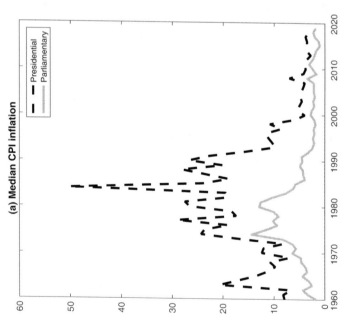

Figure 2.3 CPI inflation and the form of government.

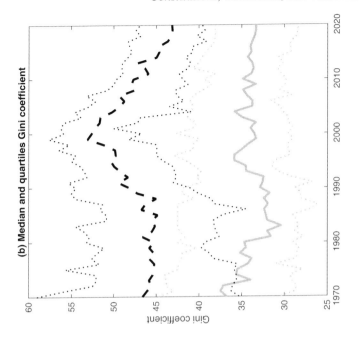

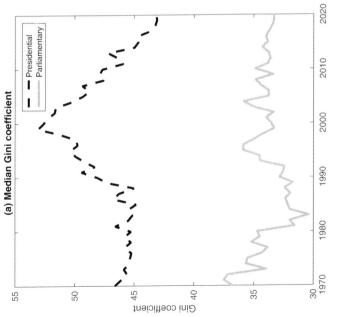

Figure 2.4 Gini coefficients and the form of government.

by comparing the proportion of income to the proportion of population across the whole distribution. An economy where everyone receives the same income would have a Gini coefficient of zero; one where all the income accrues to one individual would have a Gini coefficient of 1. High and rising values of the Gini coefficient are therefore associated with rising income inequality.

Panel (a) of Figure 2.4 presents the median values of the Gini coefficient in presidential and parliamentary countries and reveals that income inequality is higher in presidential regimes throughout the sample. Moreover, this gap widens until 2010 after which it contracts, yet remains sizable throughout the sample period. Panel (b) of Figure 2.4 additionally presents the 25th and 75th percentiles (in dotted lines of the same colour) and demonstrates that the differences in income inequality between parliamentary and presidential countries prevail across the whole distribution. Similar to the case with both GDP per capita and inflation, this finding is robust to sample variations as is clear from Figure A2.2 in the Data Appendix presenting the evolution of the Gini coefficient with different starting points.

The level and inequality of income across regimes

To further illustrate the consequences of governance systems on the economy, Figure 2.5 combines outcomes with respect to the two key indicators – GDP per capita and income inequality where parliamentary countries are represented by asterisks and presidential ones by dots. The sample averages for each variable are marked with dashed lines, splitting the sample into four quadrants: the upper (lower) left (right) holds countries with above-average (below-average) income and below-average (above-average) inequality, respectively. The best combination is contained in the top-left (high income, low inequality), and the worst is in the bottom-right (low income, high inequality) quadrant. Both the top-right and bottom-left quadrants combine one set of favourable and one set of unfavourable outcomes; higher than average income with higher than average inequality, and lower than average income and lower than average inequality, respectively. Figure 2.5 also displays the three-letter country code identifying each nation in the sample.

As can be seen from Figure 2.5, of the countries that are positioned in the top-left quarter holding the best combination of high income and low inequality, all but four are parliamentary regimes (36 of 40 countries). On the other hand, half of all presidential countries are in the bottom-right quadrant representing below-average income and above-average inequality – the worst set of outcomes. Only 38% of all presidential countries have above-average income and only 20% have below-average income inequality.

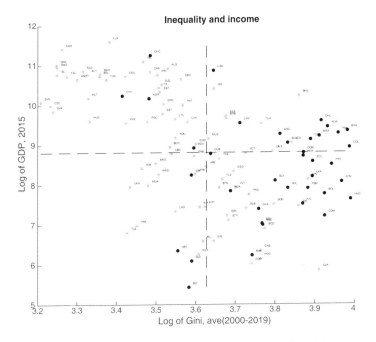

Figure 2.5 Inequality and income under parliamentary and presidential systems.

2.3 On human development indicators

In one of the most comprehensive studies on presidential regimes, Gerring *et al.* (2009) explore the implications of the form of government across a wide range of political, economic, and human development measures.[6] They utilise an extensive dataset consisting of 124 countries covering the period 1951–2000. Their findings support the argument that parliamentary regimes are more effective in delivering democratic stability and effective governance, also pointing to the clear dominance of parliamentary regimes with respect to economic development. Outcomes across human development indicators such as life expectancy and infant mortality also indicate the superiority of parliamentary systems. Furthermore, they also show that improvements achieved under parliamentary regimes regarding both economic and human development are sizable.

We now examine the relationship between government systems and human development by extending the set of metrics to include health outcomes. Utilising the World Bank database, we calculate sample averages for measures such as fertility rates, infant and maternal mortality, and life expectancy, as presented in Table 2.1. To these, we add measures of happiness from the World Values Survey.[7] Entries in Table 2.1 document the average values of human development indicators under both the presidential and parliamentary systems in our sample, using both the BG2013 (columns 1–3) and PT2003 (columns 4–6) classifications, providing fresh insights into the association between the form of government and human development and public health outcomes. In countries with presidential regimes, the fertility rate is over half a birth higher than in countries under parliamentary systems, and this difference is statistically significant. Maternal mortality is also significantly higher in presidential countries, more than double that of parliamentary countries. Further, babies born in presidential countries have a higher chance of having a low birth weight, and there is a higher infant mortality rate compared with parliamentary countries. Finally, the prevalence of adolescent fertility (measured as births to mothers aged between 15 and 19) is statistically significantly higher in countries with presidential regimes.

Table 2.1 also reveals that the life expectancy in parliamentary countries is, on average, approximately three years longer than presidential ones, and this difference is present for both females and males. There is also greater food insecurity in presidential regimes with more than twice the prevalence in parliamentary countries. Despite all this, it is estimated that those in presidential countries report higher levels of happiness compared with those in presidential countries. Finally, there is inconclusive evidence on whether presidential or parliamentary countries did better from COVID; presidential countries did better in terms of death statistics but not statistically significantly so with small differences across regime types.

Table 2.1 Human development and the form of government

Classification	BG2013			PT2003		
	(1) Pres	(2) Parl	(3) Diff	(4) Pres	(5) Parl	(6) Diff
	Panel (a): fertility					
Fertility	3.037	2.470	−0.568**	2.612	1.947	−0.665***
	0.214	0.154	0.035	0.181	0.097	0.003
	39	85		22	38	
Maternal mortality	40.778	13.979	−26.799***	38.000	9.833	−28.167***
	7.979	4.842	0.007	6.106	4.775	0.001
	18	47		12	30	
Low birth weight	10.948	8.787	−2.161**	10.059	8.466	−1.593
	0.711	0.603	0.023	0.747	0.719	0.131
	34	65		22	32	

Classification	BG2013			PT2003		
	(1) Pres	(2) Parl	(3) Diff	(4) Pres	(5) Parl	(6) Diff
Infant mortality	23.869 3.481 39	17.305 2.066 85	−6.565 0.110	15.250 1.798 22	9.061 1.630 38	−6.189** 0.014
Adolescent fertility	64.197 5.396 38	37.613 4.339 79	−26.584*** 0.000	62.476 4.837 22	20.273 3.139 38	−42.204*** 0.000
Panel (b): life expectancy						
Life expectancy	69.912 1.374 39	72.805 0.836 84	2.892* 0.077	73.461 0.979 22	76.666 0.980 38	3.205** 0.025
Life expectancy female	71.866 1.231 38	74.365 0.796 80	2.499* 0.093	74.729 0.921 22	78.193 0.877 38	3.464*** 0.009
Life expectancy male	69.305 1.163 38	71.950 0.785 80	2.645* 0.063	71.742 0.924 22	75.977 0.867 38	4.235*** 0.002
Panel (c): other health and well-being outcomes						
Food insecurity	9.838 2.658 21	3.223 0.507 48	−6.615** 0.023	7.720 1.765 15	3.130 0.770 27	−4.590** 0.028
Happiness	0.750 0.137 17	0.709 0.009 41	−0.041** 0.018	0.732 0.018 19	0.708 0.009 31	−0.024 0.241
COVID deaths	113.703 20.539 39	131.276 13.093 86	17.573 0.473	132.236 22.718 33	143.916 15.716 51	11.680 0.674

Note. Pres, Parl, and Diff denote, respectively, outcomes under the presidential and parliamentary regimes and the difference between the two. BG2013 and PT2003 are used, respectively, for Bormann and Golder's (2013) and Persson and Tabellini's (2003) classifications. For each of the variables represented in the first column, the mean is calculated under both presidential and parliamentary regimes, with both the standard error and the number of observations presented underneath; in the third and sixth columns, the difference between the means under parliamentary and presidential systems is presented, with p-values from t-tests underneath. A standard star convention is used, with *, **, and *** representing significance levels of 10%, 5%, and 1%, respectively. Both BG2013 and PT2003 are used in classifying presidential versus parliamentary regimes; in the case of the former, semi-presidential systems are not included in the analysis. Data Appendix displays the detailed description of variables and source of all data utilised in this table.

Figure 2.6 presents the same data as Table 2.1, now illustrating the distribution of these variables split between parliamentary (grey bars) and presidential (black bars) countries. The *x*-axis represents the variable described in the title of the panel, and the *y*-axis represents the proportion of the cohort in each 20% (a 'quintile'). Across the range of indicators, the differences reported in Table 2.1 are clear. What is particularly interesting is the distribution of COVID-19 deaths, where presidential regimes have outliers for both very low deaths (for example Burundi and Nicaragua) and very high deaths (specifically Peru and Brazil). Consistent with the debate in Chapter 1, presidents can be decisive and act quickly, something which was of value in mitigating the effects of COVID-19; however, this places more risk on a concentration of power where decisive but poor decision-making can lead to these bipolar results.

Health and income

To jointly examine the effects of the form of government on economic outcomes and human development, income per capita and life expectancy under the two government systems are combined in Figure 2.7 where, as earlier, parliamentary countries are represented by asterisks and presidential ones by dots. The sample averages for each variable are marked with dashed lines, splitting the data into four quadrants: the upper (lower) left (right) holds countries with above-average (below-average) income and below-average (above-average) life expectancy, respectively. The best combination is now contained in the top-right quadrant with higher-than-average incomes and higher-than-average life expectancy. Similarly, the worst pair of outcomes are contained in the bottom-left quadrant (below-average income combined with below-average life expectancy). Both the top-left and bottom-right quadrants combine one set of favourable and one set of unfavourable outcomes: higher than average income with lower than average life expectancy; and lower than average income and higher than average life expectancy, respectively.

In Figure 2.7, 50% of all parliamentary regimes sit in the best top-right quadrant. In contrast, only 35% of the presidential ones achieve this combination. Underlying this outcome, 53% of countries under parliamentary systems have above-average income as compared with only 38% of presidential regimes. Likewise, 59% of parliamentary regimes, as compared with 54% of presidential ones, have above-average life expectancy.

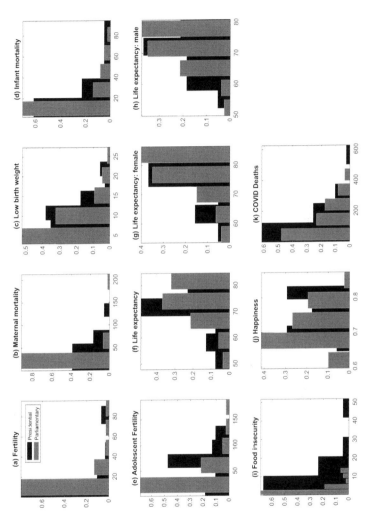

Figure 2.6 Distribution of human development indicators and the form of government.

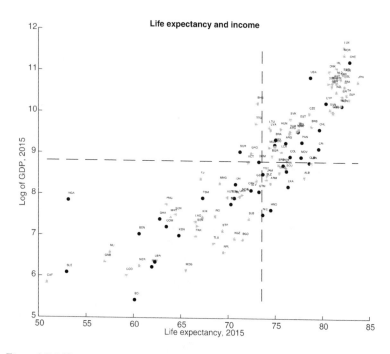

Figure 2.7 Life expectancy and income under parliamentary and presidential systems.

2.4 Conclusions

The findings of the existing literature examining the implications of presidential regimes on economic performance, as reported earlier, are consistently unfavourable. Studies comparing presidential versus parliamentary regimes clearly indicate that in countries run by presidential regimes, inferior outcomes are achieved across economic and human development spectrums. More specifically, parliamentary regimes routinely achieve higher growth, higher per capita income, lower inflation, and lower income inequality (Gerring *et al.* 2009, PT2003, Rockey 2012, MO2018). This chapter revisited these relationships by utilizing data from 138 countries over the period 1960–2019. Based on the average values across the two groups of countries, we have reaffirmed that outcomes under presidential regimes are considerably less favourable than those under parliamentary ones. First, on macroeconomic performance metrics, presidential regimes do consistently less well with lower income, higher and more volatile inflation, and significantly higher inequality. Similarly, presidential countries exhibit systematically lower human development outcomes as compared with parliamentary ones, with lower life expectancy, higher adolescent fertility, higher infant and maternal mortality, and food insecurity.

Notes

1 Cella *et al.* (2017) find that the disciplining effect of the confidence vote under the parliamentary system leads to greater efficiency in policy choice and hence improved quality of proposed policies.
2 Importantly, where possible, Cheibub *et al.* (2010) use the rules as prescribed by a country's constitution; that is, the classification is an *ex ante* rules-based approach, not dependent on the norms of historical incidence of, for example, heads of state being removed by the elected assembly.
3 Bormann and Golder (2013) update the work of Cheibub *et al.* (2010) up to and including 2016.
4 Figure 2.2 is based on a sample of 37 parliamentary and 28 presidential countries who have full sample of observations across the period. As a robustness check, Figure A2.1 in the Appendix performs the same exercise using different starting dates for data coverage.
5 Note that as CPI inflation is a rate of change year on year (and importantly not a level variable) we include all countries which have data for a given year in the sample. This means that the sample size is changing throughout Figure 2.4, but this does not add substantial noise to the results and thus does not impact potential inference. Note that this also removes the need to consider different starting dates as all countries enter when their data start.
6 See Norris (2012) for an in-depth analysis of the linkages between democratic governance and human development. Uberti and Knutsen (2021) and Knutsen (2021) also examine the role of institutions on human and economic development.
7 We take the combined dataset which includes results from both the World Values Survey and the European Values Survey to expand the number of countries in our sample.

References

Alesina, A. and Perotti, R. (1996) 'Income distribution, political instability, and investment', *European Economic Review*, 40(6), 1203–1228.
Bardhan, P. (2005) *Globalization, Inequality, and Poverty: An Overview*. University of California at Berkeley, mimeo.
Bernanke, B.S., Laubach, T., Mishkin, F.S. and Posen, A.S. (1999) *Inflation Targeting*. Princeton: Princeton University Press.
Bordo, M.D. and Meissner, C.M. (2012) 'Does inequality lead to a financial crisis?', *Journal of International Money and Finance*, 31(8), 2147–2161.

Bormann, N.-C. and Golder, M. (2013) 'Democratic electoral systems around the world, 1946–2011', *Electoral Studies*, 32(2), 360–369.

Carney, M. (2015) 'Inflation in a globalised world', Speech at Economic Policy Symposium in Jackson Hole, WY, August 2015.

Cella, M., Iannantuoni, G. and Manzoni, E. (2017) 'Do the right thing: Incentives for policy selection in presidential and parliamentary systems', *Economica*, 84(335), 430–453.

Cheibub, J.A., Gandhi, J. and Vreeland, J.R. (2010) 'Democracy and dictatorship revisited', *Public Choice*, 143(1–2), 67–101.

Ciccarelli, M. and Mojon, B. (2010) 'Global inflation', *The Review of Economics and Statistics*, 92(3), 524–535.

Claessens, S. and Perotti, E. (2007) 'Finance and inequality: Channels and evidence', *Journal of Comparative Economics*, 35(4), 748–773.

Easterly, W. and Rebelo, S. (1993) 'Fiscal policy and economic growth', *Journal of Monetary Economics*, 32(3), 417–458.

Galor, O. and Moav, O. (2004) 'From physical to human capital accumulation: Inequality and the process of development', *The Review of Economic Studies*, 71(4), 1001–1026.

Gerring, J., Thacker, S.C. and Moreno, C. (2009) 'Are parliamentary systems better?', *Comparative Political Studies*, 42(3), 327–359.

Ha, J., Kose, M.A. and Ohnsorge, F. (eds.) (2019) *Inflation in Emerging and Developing Economies: Evolution, Drivers, and Policies*. Washington, DC: World Bank Publications.

Kamber, G. and Wong, B. (2020) 'Global factors and trend inflation', *Journal of International Economics*, 122, 103265.

King, M. (2005) 'What has inflation targeting achieved?', *The Inflation Targeting Debate*, 11–16.

Knutsen, C.H. (2011) 'Which democracies prosper? Electoral rules, form of government and economic growth', *Electoral Studies*, 30(1), 83–90.

Knutsen, C.H. (2021). 'Autocracy and variations in economic development outcomes'. In Crawford, Gordon & Abdulai, Abdul-Gafaru (Ed.), *Research Handbook on Democracy and Development*. Edward Elgar.

McManus, R. and Ozkan, F.G. (2018) 'Who does better for the economy? Presidents versus parliamentary democracies', *Public Choice*, 176, 361–387.

Milanovic, B. (2018) 'Why inequality matters?', VoxEU, available at https://voxeu.org/content/why-inequality-matters.

Mishkin, F.S. (2001) *From Monetary Targeting to Inflation Targeting (No. 2684)*. Washington, DC: World Bank Publications.

Mumtaz, H. and Surico, P. (2012) 'Evolving international inflation dynamics: World and country-specific factors', *Journal of the European Economic Association*, 10(4), 716–734.

Norris, P. (2012) *Making Democratic Governance Work: How Regimes Shape Prosperity, Welfare, and Peace*. Cambridge: Cambridge University Press.

Panizza, U. (2002) 'Income inequality and economic growth: Evidence from American data', *Journal of Economic Growth*, 7(1), 25–41.

Persson, T. and Tabellini, G. (2003) *The Economic Effects of Constitutions*. Cambridge: MA: The MIT Press.

Piketty, T. (2003) 'Income inequality in France, 1901–1998', *Journal of Political Economy*, 111(5), 1004–1042.

Piketty, T. and Saez, E. (2003) 'Income inequality in the United States, 1913–1998', *The Quarterly Journal of Economics*, 118(1), 1–41.

Rajan, R. (2010) 'How inequality fueled the crisis', *Project Syndicate*, 9.

Rockey, J. (2012) 'Reconsidering the fiscal effects of constitutions', *European Journal of Political Economy*, 28(3), 313–323.

Shugart, M.S. (1999) 'Presidentialism, parliamentarism, and the provision of collective goods in less-developed countries', *Constitutional Political Economy*, 10(1), 53–88.

Stiglitz, J.E. (2012) 'Macroeconomic fluctuations, inequality, and human development', *Journal of Human Development and Capabilities*, 13(1), 31–58.

Svensson, L.E. (2010) 'Inflation targeting', in *Handbook of Monetary Economics*. Vol. 3. Elsevier, pp. 1237–1302.

Uberti, L.J. and Knutsen, C.H. (2021) 'Institutions, human capital and economic growth', in E. Douarin and O. Havrylyshyn (eds.), *The Palgrave Handbook of Comparative Economics*. Palgrave Macmillan. ISBN: 978-3-030-50887-6.

Van Treeck, T. (2014) 'Did inequality cause the US financial crisis?', *Journal of Economic Surveys*, 28(3), 421–448.

3 Forms of government and political, legal, and economic institutions

The previous chapter provided an overview of the relationship between constitutional rules and macroeconomic outcomes by revisiting the existing work on the economic effects of government systems. Parallel to the existing relevant literature, work in Chapter 2 focussed on two dimensions of how government systems influence economic performance: (*i*) on macroeconomic performance and (*ii*) on human and economic development. Our analysis in Chapter 2 provided additional support for the previous findings that presidential regimes are consistently associated with worse economic and health outcomes on a wide range of metrics, from income per capita to life expectancy.

Having examined the link between the constitutional form and economic outcomes, (represented by line A in Figure 1.1), we now turn to the mechanisms through which the former shapes the latter – the core interest in this book. As is set out in detail in Chapter 1, our hypothesis is that institutions are the main channels through which government form impacts economic outcomes. In the remainder of this book, we execute our analysis of *how* the former affects the latter in three stages. First, we examine how government systems influence institutions, studying the differences in political, legal, and economic institutions under presidential versus parliamentary systems (as represented by lines B and C in Figure 1.1) taken up in this chapter, and more formally in Chapter 4. In the second stage, we focus on the impact of institutions on economic outcomes, uncovering how those outcomes differ under presidential versus parliamentary regimes, to the extent that institutions differ under the two as investigated in the first stage. In the third stage, we incorporate the possibility that government systems can impact outcomes both *directly*, line A, and *indirectly* through their role in shaping institutions, lines B and C, and in turn, the role of institutions shaping economic outcomes, lines D and E. Both the second and third stages are taken up in Chapter 4.

DOI: 10.4324/9781003141242-3

In order to evaluate the consequences of presidential versus parliamentary regimes, it is crucial to understand the wider institutional context in which they operate (see, for example, Elgie 2005, Kedar 2005, and Carey 2008). In what follows, we present a set of arguments drawn from the existing literature mapping the features of the institutional structure to economic performance and set out how we approach them in our empirical analysis.

3.1 Institutional characteristics

The nature and the quality of democracy

It has long been recognised that both the form and the quality of democracy play a key role in political and economic outcomes. In a highly influential piece, Lijphart (1984) carefully distinguishes between consensus and majoritarian democracies, which are characterised by, respectively, inclusive and compromising features versus exclusive and competitive ones. As such, consensus democracies are seen as a *kinder and gentler* form of governance, where '*as many people as possible will do the governing*'. Clearly, consensus democracies imply wider representation and broader participation, especially of minorities (Lijphart 1994, Anderson and Guillory 1997, Bormann 2010). Indeed, Lijphart (2012) finds that consensus democracies have a better record across several macroeconomic performance metrics. Yet, conventional wisdom points to a potentially favourable effect of majoritarian democracies on economic performance on account of decisive and more effective policy-making that is argued to be their defining feature. Overall, the form of democracy is seen as a crucial determinant of economic performance, a proposition also put forward by Persson (2005).

The quality and the inclusiveness of institutions

Beyond the nature and the quality of democracy, the quality and the inclusiveness of institutions are also regarded as important channels through which governance impacts policy. Indeed, the role of institutions on various political and economic outcomes has been one of the most widely explored issues in economics since the 1990s (see, for example, Rodrik *et al.* 2004, Acemoglu 2005 and 2010, Acemoglu and Johnson 2005, North 2005a, 2005b, and Acemoglu and Robinson 2008 among many others). The quality of institutions within which individual government systems operate would also be expected to impact the economic consequences of presidential versus parliamentary regimes. For example, authoritarian regimes with limited public deliberation are found to result in inferior outcomes (Chandra and Rudra 2015).

Legislative power and control

Given the powerful nature of the presidential office, the strength of the checks and balances is expected to play a key role in mitigating the potential harmful effects of presidentialism (Shugart and Carey 1992). For example, checks and balances constrain the winner-takes-all tendencies inherent in presidential systems (Mainwaring and Shugart 1997, Henisz 2004, Alt and Lassen 2008). It is not surprising, therefore, that the separation of power among different office holders, creating checks and balances is seen as a key feature of successful presidencies. This suggests that the distribution of power matters: in systems where presidents hold only limited power over legislation or a lack of veto power may produce more preferential outcomes for presidential regimes.

Electoral system and the number of parties

Whether a presidential regime operates with a two or multiparty system is viewed as another important characteristic impacting its viability. Presidentialism with a fractional multiparty system is seen as a particularly difficult combination and an obstacle to stable democracy (see, for example, Mainwaring 1993 and Mainwaring and Shugart 1997). This argument is based on the premise that multipartism makes it more difficult for the president to be involved in effective dialogue on policy issues and to build inter-party coalitions. A greater number of parties is also expected to increase ideological polarization and the likelihood of executive/legislative deadlock. Electoral systems restricting the number of parties are therefore expected to improve outcomes under presidential systems. This is likely to be the case under majoritarian single-district electoral rules rather than with proportional representation.

Economic institutions and quality of economic policies

Economic institutions establish property rights and rules of exchange and facilitate transactions and cooperation among agents and thus play a crucial role in outcomes. Economic institutions may take the form of land tenure, patents, competition policy, employment regulations, budgetary processes, stock exchanges, central banking, and regulatory institutions. Societies where there are secure property rights, where starting a business is easy and straightforward, and where tax rules are transparent and not prohibitive are more likely to deliver higher investment, greater innovation, and hence stronger macroeconomic performance (see, for example, Glaeser *et al.* 2004, Rodrik 2004, Acemoglu and Johnson 2005, Helpman 2008, and Tabellini 2008).

3.2 Empirical results

The quality of democracy

To formally consider the hypothesis that the nature and quality of democracy systematically differ between parliamentary and presidential countries, we look at differences across five variables. The variable *Polity* combines assessments of both how authoritarian (to what extent is political participation discouraged and the chief executive exercises power without constraint) and how democratic a regime is (to what extent can the electorate express their political preferences, exercise civil liberties, and are institutions in place to govern this). *Polity* is measured on a $(-10,10)$ scale where higher values denote more democratic and less authoritarian regimes.[1] We also utilise *Durable* which represents the length of time in which the *Polity* score has been continuously positive, indicating how long a country has been operating within a democracy.

The *Varieties of Democracy* database also provides information on the nature of democracy within countries, looking beyond the operation of elections and focussing on five high-level principles of democracy: electoral, liberal, participatory, deliberative, and egalitarian.[2] We utilise *ElecDem* which measures the extent to which political and civil organisations can operate freely and elections can be free of fraud; *ElecDem* is bounded by zero where higher values represent greater levels of electoral democracy. We also include a measure of the perceptions of political stability (*PolStab*) and a measure of the perceptions of the electorate regarding the ability to select their government (*Voice*); both of which are obtained from the *Worldwide Governance Indicators* of the World Bank. Table 3.1 documents the average values of our quality of democracy variables (amongst others, as discussed later) under both the presidential and parliamentary systems in our sample, using both the BG2013 and PT2003 classifications, as adopted earlier. A full description of all variables is provided in the Data Appendix.

As illustrated in Table 3.1, there is systematic variation in the nature and quality of democracy across the two forms of government. Presidential regimes are associated with consistently lower scores of democracy. For all five measures and in both classifications, parliamentary regimes feature higher levels of democracy, longer continual periods of democracy, higher levels of participation in electoral democracies, and greater political

Table 3.1 Presidential and parliamentary regimes: democratic, societal, and institutional metrics

Classification	BG2013			PT2003		
	(1) Pres	(2) Parl	(3) Diff	(4) Pres	(5) Parl	(6) Diff
	Panel (a): nature and quality of democracy					
Polity	2.723 3.722 36	4.806 5.017 69	2.083*** 0.009	3.255 0.629 33	6.541 0.576 46	3.286*** 0.000
Durable	35.694 35.286 36	39.343 38.659 67	3.649 0.315	36.424 6.010 33	54.804 6.460 46	8.823** 0.041
ElecDem	0.463 0.175 37	0.573 0.238 72	0.110*** 0.004	0.473 0.029 33	0.671 0.029 48	0.199*** 0.000
PolStab	−0.248 0.816 39	0.327 0.905 82	0.575*** 0.000	−0.277 0.135 33	0.509 0.112 50	0.786*** 0.000
Voice	0.091 0.692 39	0.547 0.821 82	0.456*** 0.001	0.009 0.127 33	0.839 0.090 50	0.830*** 0.000
	Panel (b): society					
MediaFree	0.733 0.560 37	1.028 0.732 71	0.295** 0.011	0.797 0.103 33	1.296 0.108 46	0.499*** 0.001
CivicSoc	0.601 0.174 37	0.656 0.212 72	0.055* 0.076	0.594 0.030 33	0.735 0.027 48	0.140*** 0.001
CivLib	0.614 0.166 37	0.733 0.209 72	0.119*** 0.001	0.621 0.028 33	0.808 0.023 48	0.187*** 0.000
FreeExp	0.679 0.267 37	0.782 0.269 71	0.103** 0.031	0.690 0.042 33	0.854 0.034 46	0.164*** 0.003
	Panel (c): quality and the inclusiveness of institutions					
GovtEff	−0.225 0.794 39	0.389 0.982 81	0.613*** 0.000	−0.125 0.134 33	0.908 0.119 50	1.034*** 0.000

Classification	BG2013			PT2003		
	(1) Pres	(2) Parl	(3) Diff	(4) Pres	(5) Parl	(6) Diff
RegQual	−0.167	0.390	0.557***	−0.056	0.866	0.921***
	0.786	0.914	0.000	0.136	0.107	0.000
	39	81		33	50	
PartDem	0.298	0.376	0.078***	0.304	0.446	0.142***
	0.143	0.191	0.009	0.025	0.025	0.000
	37	72		33	48	

Note: For each of the variables represented in the first column, the mean is calculated under both presidential and parliamentary regimes, with both the standard error and the number of observations presented underneath; in the third and sixth columns, the difference between these two means is presented, with p-values from t-tests presented underneath. A standard star convention is used, with *, **, and *** representing significance levels of 10%, 5%, and 1%, respectively. Both BG2013 and PT2003 are used in classifying presidential versus parliamentary regimes; in the case of the former, semi-presidential systems are not included in the analysis.

stability and democratic agency. Moreover, the age of democracy is the only variable for which the differences are not statistically significant, but only under the BG2013 classification; for the other four variables, parliamentary countries are observed to have better, more inclusive, and free democracies than presidential countries, and these differences are statistically significant at typically 99% confidence. Overall, with respect to the quality of democratic institutions, the data provide a clear distinction between parliamentary and presidential institutions in favour of the former.

Figure 3.1 presents the same data as Table 3.1, now illustrating the distribution of these variables split between parliamentary (grey bars) and presidential (black bars) countries. Similar to earlier, the x-axis represents the variable described in the title of the panel, and the y-axis represents the proportion of the cohort in each quantile. For the variables in which there is a statistically significant difference, the results are striking, with parliamentary countries clustering at the highest (favourable) end of outcomes, and presidential ones at the lowest end.

Society

Naturally, it is possible that beyond direct democratic norms and institutions, there may be differences in other aspects of these societies, through which the form of government may have an impact. We therefore examine four additional variables – again from the *Varieties of Democracy* database discussed earlier. Of these, *CivicSoc* is a measure of the degree to which policymakers consult society. *CivLib* is a measure of the degree to which

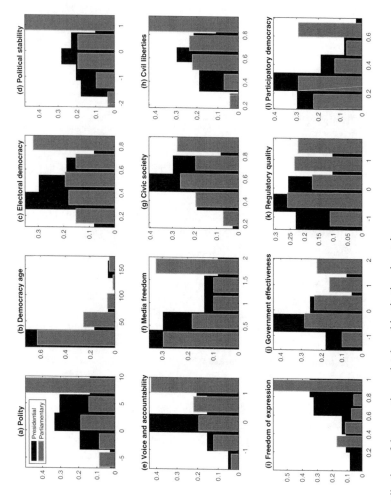

Figure 3.1 Distribution of democratic, societal, and institutional metrics.

civil liberties are respected in a country such as the absence of both violence committed by government agents and constraints on private liberties. *Free-Exp* measures media and press freedoms within a country, and *MediaFree* measures the degree to which media is free from government intervention: a variable ranging from zero to four, with higher values representing greater media freedom. *SocPart*, *CivLib*, and *FreeExp* are all measures bounded by zero and one with higher values representing higher degrees of participation, civil liberties, and freedom of expression, respectively.

Panel (b) of Table 3.1 presents the differences in these three variables across presidential and parliamentary countries. On average, parliamentary countries are seen to exhibit greater media freedoms, more extensive civic society, civil liberties, and freedom of expression compared to presidential countries. Moreover, these differences are consistently statistically significant. Panels (f)–(i) of Figure 3.1 presents the data in panel (b) of Table 3.2, now looking at the distribution of these variables across the cohorts. For civic society, civil liberties, and freedom of expression, a majority of parliamentary countries have the maximum possible value, whereas presidential countries are located at best in the middle of the range of scores. As with other panels in Figure 3.1, the evidence points in a similar direction, with values being close to the maximum possible for parliamentary countries but more spread and towards the lowest end of scores for presidential nations.

Table 3.2 Presidential and parliamentary regimes: legislative, electoral, and economic institutional metrics

Classification	BG2013			PT2003		
	(1) Pres	(2) Parl	(3) Diff	(4) Pres	(5) Parl	(6) Diff
	Panel (a): legislative power and control					
RuleOfLaw	−0.281	0.434	0.715***	−0.253	0.855	1.109***
	0.821	0.958	0.000	0.147	0.121	0.000
	39	81		33	50	
Xconst	2.087	3.623	1.536*	3.011	5.484	2.473***
	4.067	5.965	0.062	0.465	0.291	0.000
	36	69		33	46	
PolCon	0.240	0.319	0.078***	0.250	0.367	0.116***
	0.105	0.147	0.001	0.017	0.018	0.000
	36	80		32	51	

(Continued)

Table 3.2 (Continued)

Classification	BG2013			PT2003		
	(1) Pres	(2) Parl	(3) Diff	(4) Pres	(5) Parl	(6) Diff
JudCon	0.511	0.684	0.172***	0.543	0.776	0.232***
	0.248	0.239	0.000	0.041	0.028	0.000
	37	71		33	46	
CorrCon	−0.256	0.401	0.65***	−0.208	0.845	1.054***
	0.794	1.034	0.000	0.147	0.141	0.000
	39	81		33	50	
	Panel (b): electoral system and the number of parties					
Parties	4.330	3.945	−0.386	3.963	4.084	0.121
	2.074	1.463	0.312	0.298	0.204	0.738
	37	81		27	48	
Majoritarian	0.311	0.433	0.122	0.222	0.384	0.162
	0.446	0.480	0.174	0.222	0.384	0.162
	38	87		27	48	
	Panel (c): economic institutions					
Education	5.991	7.584	1.593***	6.263	8.069	1.806***
	2.291	2.716	0.005	0.421	0.340	0.002
	30	38		27	36	
Openness	64.380	86.598	22.219***	57.863	89.369	31.507***
	36.834	47.156	0.006	4.380	7.842	0.001
	39	79		33	50	
ExRateVol	370.810	121.140	−249.670	264.619	23.523	−241.096*
	939.907	479.729	0.124	627.134	73.343	0.087
	39	82		22	38	
CBI	0.469	0.445	−0.025	0.452	0.408	−0.044
	0.157	0.122	0.473	0.030	0.017	0.204
	27	62		29	46	
HumanCapital	2.021	2.503	0.482***	2.108	2.611	0.503***
	0.522	0.701	0.000	0.093	0.082	0.000
	34	63		32	49	
Government consumption	13.756	19.022	5.265***	12.907	17.467	4.560***
	1.461	1.200	0.007	0.570	0.607	0.000
	36	74		32	49	
Tax revenue	18.888	30.435	11.547***	19.678	29.567	9.889***
	1.009	2.375	0.000	1.174	1.267	0.000
	31	74		30	51	
Debt	46.880	54.650	7.770	48.662	54.106	5.444
	5.648	5.154	0.314	6.112	6.204	0.535
	23	49		22	39	

Note. Similar to Table 3.1, now displaying differences in *legislative, electoral, and economic institutions* related metrics across the two systems of government.

The quality and the inclusiveness of institutions

To consider further the hypothesis that the quality and inclusiveness of institutions is a potential channel through which parliamentary countries perform better economically than presidential ones, we look at differences in three variables across the two regimes. *GovtEff* and *RegQual* measure perceptions of government effectiveness (provision of goods and services and formation of policies) and regulatory quality (ability to formulate and implement good qualities allowing for the development of the private sector), respectively. Both *GovtEff* and *RegQual* are obtained from the *Worldwide Governance Indicators* from the World Bank and range between −3 and 2. Moreover, from the *Varieties of Democracy* database, we utilise *PartDem* which measures the level to which democracy is participatory within a country, looking at participation and engagement of the electorate at a subnational level. *PartDem* is bounded by zero and one where higher values represent greater levels of participation. Panel (c) of Table 3.1 presents differences in these variables between parliamentary and presidential regimes, using a similar format to that in panels (a) and (b).

There is clear evidence to suggest that parliamentary countries are associated with higher levels of government effectiveness, the quality of regulation, and participatory democracy; moreover, for all three variables, these differences are statistically significant at 99% confidence level. Panels (j)–(l) of Figure 3.1 present the data in panel (c) of Table 3.2, now looking at the distribution of these variables across the cohorts. As with other panels in Figure 3.1, the evidence points in a similar direction, with values being close to the maximum possible for parliamentary countries but more spread and towards the lowest end of scores for presidential nations.

Legislative power and control

Regarding the differences in legislative power and control between the two regimes, we look at differences across five variables. *RuleOfLaw* measures agents' perceived confidence in the rule of law of a country, over contract enforcement, property rights, the police, and the courts, and range between −3 and 2, also obtained from the *Worldwide Governance Indicators*. From the Polity IV database, we utilise *Xconst* which is a measure of constraints ('checks and balances') on the chief executive of a government, a variable ranging from one to seven, with higher values representing the greater scale of constraints. Furthermore, from the *Political Constraint* (POLCON) database, we take measures of legislative control (*PolCon*) which measures the feasibility of policy change incorporating both the number of independent branches of government with veto control and the extent to which these branches align; and judicial constraints (*JudCon*) a measure of fractionalisation of the judicial process.[3] Both of these variables range from zero to one with higher values representing greater degrees of constraint. Finally, we include a measure of perceived corruption control, defined as the degree to which public power is free from influence to promote private gain (*CorrCon*); values range between −3 and 2, also obtained from the *Worldwide Governance Indicators*.

Panel (a) of Table 3.2 is similar to that of Table 3.1 and illustrates that for all five variables, parliamentary countries perform better than presidential ones and that in nine out of ten cases (five variables measured across two different classifications of government systems), these differences are statistically significant frequently at 99%. Specifically, parliamentary regimes are associated with higher levels of perceived confidence in the rule of law, constraints on leaders through both political and legal channels, and better (perceived) control of corruption in policy-making.[4] Panels (a)–(e) of Figure 3.2 present the distribution of these variables illustrating high levels of rule of law, checks and balances (*XConst*), and judicial constraints as well as the perception of lower control over corruption in presidential countries. Similar to Figure 3.1, the differences across the two types of countries are clearly observable.[5]

Electoral system and the number of parties

To explore the hypothesis that the electoral system is a potential channel through which parliamentary countries perform better economically than presidential ones, we look at differences across two variables both of which are taken from BG2013; the effective number of *Parties* operating in an election, where the effectiveness of a given party is determined by the vote share they receive; and where the voting system is *Majoritarian* as opposed to proportional representation. Results are presented in panel (b) of Table 3.2, with presidential regimes being associated with a similar number of parties and with a lower likelihood of (but statistically insignificant) majoritarian electoral systems. To put differently, although the electoral process may influence macroeconomic outcomes, there is no systematic difference in these processes between countries governed by presidential and parliamentary regimes. It is also clear from panels (f) and (g) of Figure 3.2 that there is no clear difference in electoral systems across the two forms of government in our sample.

Economic institutions

A more direct way in which the form of government might influence macroeconomic outcomes is through economic institutions, both with respect to policy setting and through the impact of those policies. To test this

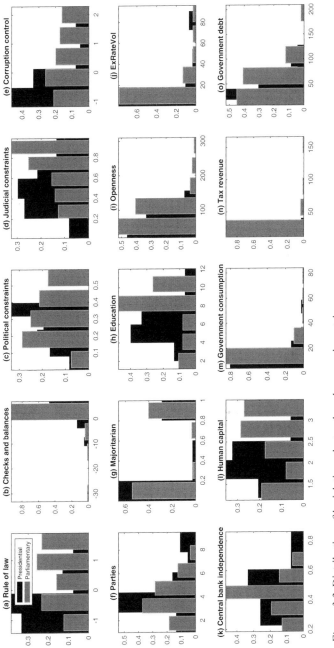

Figure 3.2 Distribution of legislative, electoral, and economic metrics.

hypothesis, we consider differences across a set of variables that can be viewed as proxies for economic institutions. As a measure of the differences in the workforce, we utilise *Education* and *HumanCapital*, the former of which measures the mean of the total number of years of education (taken from Barro and Lee 2013) and the latter is an index of human capital per person, based on both years of schooling and returns to education (obtained from the Penn World Table). We also consider the *Openness* of the economy, measured as the volume of external trade – the sum of imports and exports – expressed as a proportion of GDP (data obtained from the World Bank), as well as the standard deviation of the nominal exchange rate (against the US dollar; again, data obtained from World Bank). We utilise an index of central bank independence (*CBI*) measuring the degree to which monetary and financial policy is conducted without the oversight of politicians.[6] We also obtain from the World Bank variables on government finances; final government expenditure as a proportion of GDP (*GovtCons*), tax revenue as a proportion of GDP (*TaxRev*), and central government debt as a proportion of GDP (*Debt*).

Panel (c) of Table 3.2 presents results like those discussed earlier, where it is observed that countries with a parliamentary regime have higher levels of schooling, human capital, and openness to trade. Presidential countries are observed to exhibit higher levels of exchange rate volatility (although this is only statistically significant using the BG2013 classification for the forms of government). Interestingly, presidential countries are also seen to have higher levels of *CBI*, although these differences are only statistically significant under the PT2003 classification. Parliamentary countries are observed to have higher levels of government consumption, tax revenue, and government debt; however, with respect to the latter, this is not statistically significant.

Panels (h)–(o) of Figure 3.2 present the distribution of these variables revealing the better performance of parliamentary compared to presidential countries with respect to human capital, education, and openness. Higher rates of exchange rate volatility under presidential regimes are also evident from panel (k), although differences in government finances are less stark.

Semi-presidential regimes

The analysis in this chapter so far has looked at the differences between those countries classified as parliamentary and presidential in both the PT2003 and BG2013 classifications; however, as discussed in Chapter 2, there are also 'semi-presidential' regimes where a popularly elected president can be removed by the assembly; 31 countries in our sample are defined as such in 2015. Existing work on semi-presidentialism distinguishes between premier-presidential versus president-parliamentary systems, originally suggested by Shugart and Carey (1992). This distinction is based on whether the president has the power to dismiss the cabinet and the assembly in which case the regime is classified as a presidential-parliamentary one (Russia). In premier-presidential regimes, such as France and Portugal, the president appoints the cabinet, but only the assembly may remove it through a vote of no confidence although in both regimes president is elected by popular vote. Consistent with the findings on presidential regimes being more prone to democratic instability, president parliamentarism is found to be less conducive to democracy than premier-presidential regimes (see, for example, Elgie 2020).

In our analysis, we observe that with respect to the nature and quality of democracy, semi-presidential regimes sit between the presidential and parliamentary countries for all variables; however, these countries tend to be younger democracies and are associated with lower degrees of media freedom. Similarly, with societal and the quality of institutions variables [panels (b) and (c) of Table 3.1], semi-presidential outcomes are positioned between those of the two regimes; that is, they appear as a weighted average of the two polar forms of government. Semi-presidential regimes do tend to have both higher *CBI*, on average, and lower exchange rate volatility, as well as being less likely to feature majoritarian electoral systems relative to parliamentary regimes. In line with our findings, Sedelius and Linde (2018) also show that the greater the presidential power in semi-presidential regimes, the worse the democratic and economic performance.

The weight of evidence in our analysis in this chapter points to semi-presidential governments performing better than presidential regimes and worse than parliamentary ones across the outcomes discussed earlier; however, this is less conclusive than the clear differences present in comparing parliamentary and presidential forms of government, where the evidence from Tables 3.1 and 3.2 and Figures 3.1 and 3.2 is clear and concise. That is, countries operating a parliamentary regime are associated with better forms of democracy, more open and free societies, stronger institutions with a dispersion of power and control, and a stronger macroeconomic framework.

3.3 Conclusions

This chapter examined the differences across a wide range of institutional variables under parliamentary and presidential regimes with respect to the quality of democracy, government effectiveness, legislative and electoral systems, and economic governance. We found that parliamentary systems consistently feature better-quality institutions. More specifically, parliamentary countries are associated with longer continual periods of democracy, greater democratic participation and democratic agency, greater media free-doms, and more extensive civil liberties than presidential countries. Further-more, parliamentary regimes exhibit greater levels of checks and balances and judicial controls on the executive. There are also statistically significant differences between the two forms of government across metrics such as level of schooling, openness to trade, and corruption control. Importantly, parliamentary systems are associated with better schooling and human capital, greater corruption control, and greater openness to international trade, with important implications for economic outcomes.

Notes

1 www.systemicpeace.org/inscr/p5manualv2018.pdf.
2 www.v-dem.net/media/filer_public/e6/d2/e6d27595-9d69-4312-b09f-63d2
   a0a65df2/vem_codebook_v9.pdf.
3 Data on these indicators are collected from the Varieties of Democracy database, available at www.v-dem.net/.
4 Gerring and Thacker (2004) similarly establish that parliamentarism is associated with lower levels of corruption.
5 Using data from 35 emerging democracies, Andrews and Montinola (2004) also find that the rule of law is weaker under presidential regimes than parliamentary systems.
6 It has long been recognised that better macroeconomic outcomes can be achieved with independent policymakers whom the public perceive to be more credible (Kydland and Prescott 1977, Barro and Gordon 1983, Rogoff 1985, Alesina and Summers 1993, Cecchetti and Krause 2002). Cukierman *et al.* (1992) demon-strate that there can be a difference between the stated and actual levels of central bank independence.

References

Acemoglu, D. (2005) 'Constitutions, politics, and economics: A review essay on Persson and Tabellini's The economic effects of constitutions', *Journal of Economic Literature*, 43, 1025–1048.
Acemoglu, D. (2010) 'Growth and institutions', in *Economic Growth*. London: Palgrave Macmillan, pp. 107–115.
Acemoglu, D. and Johnson, S. (2005) 'Unbundling institutions', *Journal of Political Economy*, 113(5), 949–995.
Acemoglu, D. and Robinson, J. (2008) *The Role of Institutions in Growth and Development*. Vol. 10. Washington, DC: World Bank.
Alesina, A. and Summers, L.H. (1993) 'Central bank independence and macroeconomic performance: Some comparative evidence', *Journal of Money, Credit and Banking*, 25(2), 151–162.
Alt, J.E. and Lassen, D.D. (2008) 'Political and judicial checks on corruption: Evidence from American state governments', *Economics & Politics*, 20(1), 33–61.

Anderson, C.J. and Guillory, C.A. (1997) 'Political institutions and satisfaction with democracy: A cross-national analysis of consensus and majoritarian systems', *American Political Science Review*, 91(1), 66–81.

Andrews, J.T. and Montinola, G.R. (2004) 'Veto players and the rule of law in emerging democracies', *Comparative Political Studies*, 37(1), 55–87.

Barro, R. and Gordon, D.B. (1983) 'Rules, discretion and reputation in a model of monetary policy', *Journal of Monetary Economics,* 12(1), 101–121.

Barro, R. and Lee, J.W. (2013) 'A new data set of educational attainment in the world, 1950–2010', *Journal of Development Economics,* 104, 184–198.

Bormann, N.-C. (2010) 'Patterns of democracy and its critics', *Living Reviews in Democracy*, 2.

Carey, J.M. (2008) 'Presidential versus parliamentary government', in *Handbook of New Institutional Economics*. Berlin, Heidelberg: Springer, pp. 91–122.

Cecchetti, S.G. and Krause, S. (2002) 'Central bank structure, policy efficiency, and macroeconomic performance: Exploring empirical relationships', *Review-Federal Reserve Bank of Saint Louis*, 84(4), 47–60.

Chandra, S. and Rudra, N. (2015) 'Reassessing the links between regime type and economic performance: Why some authoritarian regimes show stable growth and others do not', *British Journal of Political Science*, 45(2), 253–285.

Cukierman, A., Web, S. and Neyapti, B. (1992) 'Measuring the independence of central banks and its effect on policy outcomes', *World Bank Economic Review*, 6(3), 353–398.

Elgie, R. (2005) 'From Linz to Tsebelis: Three waves of presidential/parliamentary studies?', *Democratization*, 12(1), 106–122.

Elgie, R. (2020) 'An intellectual history of the concepts of premier-presidentialism and president-parliamentarism', *Political Studies Review*, 18(1), 12–29.

Gerring, J. and Thacker, S.C. (2004) 'Political institutions and corruption: The role of unitarism and parliamentarism', *British Journal of Political Science*, 34(2), 295–330.

Glaeser, E.L., La Porta, R., Lopez-de-Silanes, F. and Shleifer, A. (2004) 'Do institutions cause growth?', *Journal of Economic Growth*, 9(3), 271–303.

Helpman, E. (ed.) (2008) *Institutions and Economic Performance*. Harvard University Press. ISBN: 9780674030770.

Henisz, W.J. (2004) 'Political institutions and policy volatility', *Economics & Politics*, 16(1), 1–27.

Kedar, O. (2005) 'When moderate voters prefer extreme parties: Policy balancing in parliamentary elections', *American Political Science Review*, 99(2), 185–199.

Kydland, F. and Prescott, E. (1977) 'Rules rather than discretion: The inconsistency of optimal plans', *Journal of Political Economy*, 85(3), 473–492.

Lijphart, A. (1984) *Democracies: Patterns of Majoritarian & Consensus Government in Twenty-one Countries*. New Haven: Yale University Press.

Lijphart, A. (1994) 'Democracies: Forms, performance, and constitutional engineering', *European Journal of Political Research*, 25(1), 1–17.

Lijphart, A. (2012) *Patterns of Democracy: Government Forms and Performance in Thirty-six Countries*. New Haven: Yale University Press.

Mainwaring, S. (1993) 'Presidentialism, multipartisanism, and democracy the difficult combination', *Comparative Political Studies*, 26(2), 198–228, available at www.rug.nl/ggdc/productivity/pwt/?langen

Mainwaring, S. and Shugart, M.S. (1997) 'Juan Linz, Presidentialism, and democracy: A critical appraisal', *Comparative Politics*, 29(4), 449–471.

North, D.C. (2005a) *Understanding the Process of Economic Change*. Princeton: Princeton University Press.

North, D.C. (2005b) 'Institutions and the performance of economics over time', in C. Ménard and M.M. Shirley (eds.), *Handbook of New Institutional Economics*. Dordrecht: Springer, pp. 21–30.

Persson, T. (2005) 'Forms of democracy, policy and economic development', Technical report, National Bureau of Economic Research.

Rodrik, D. (2004) 'Institutions and economic performance-getting institutions right', *CESIfo DICE Report*, 2(2), 10–15.

Rodrik, D., Subramanian, A. and Trebbi, F. (2004) 'Institutions rule: The primacy of institutions over geography and integration in economic development', *Journal of Economic Growth*, 9(2), 131–165.

Rogoff, K. (1985) 'The optimal degree of commitment to an intermediate monetary target', *The Quarterly Journal of Economics*, 100(4), 1169–1189.

Sedelius, T. and Linde, J. (2018) 'Unravelling semi-presidentialism: Democracy and government performance in four distinct regime types', *Democratization*, 25(1), 136–157.

Shugart, M.S. and Carey, J. (1992) *Presidents and Assemblies: Constitutional Design and Electoral Dynamics*. Cambridge: Cambridge University Press.

Tabellini, G. (2008) 'Institutions and culture', *Journal of the European Economic Association*, 6(2–3), 255–294.

4 How do constitutions influence macroeconomic outcomes?

4.1 Introduction

Having established that there are consistent differences across a wide spectrum of institutions under parliamentary and presidential systems, we can now re-examine the link between the form of government and economic performance. We do this by following an empirical methodology that explicitly incorporates the role of institutions in both economic performance and the economic effects of government systems.

The challenge in estimating the impact of government systems on macroeconomic outcomes is that the former may not be independent of the latter. For example, are presidential countries poorer than parliamentary ones because of their form of government, or is it that these countries have a presidential structure *because* they are poorer? One could imagine a situation where the decisiveness of a president (as discussed in Chapter 1) is more beneficial to poor countries and thus poorer countries *chose* to have presidential structures. This would yield a very different interpretation of the desirability of presidential regimes.

Central to this debate is whether we can consider constitutions as truly random and independent of the outcomes we want to evaluate. In theory, one way to navigate this would be to randomly allocate political structures to countries and assess outcomes; the fact that the initial allocation was random would remove any concerns of 'reverse casualty'. This may be possible in a laboratory, but not in practice. It can still be argued that constitutions may be independent of economic outcomes because for a majority of countries, the regime choice was made many years ago and has not been altered subsequently. Indeed, as documented in Table A4.1 in the Data Appendix and stated in Chapter 1, very few countries, especially among the established democracies, change their government system. When changes take place, this is usually in countries coming in and out of dictatorships.[1]

DOI: 10.4324/9781003141242-4

In principle, there are two main tools that can be used to mitigate the issues that would arise from a potential two-way relationship between government systems and economic outcomes – propensity score matching and instrumental variable estimations. By using propensity score matching, one seeks to find a pair (or more) of countries that have a similar probability of picking the same constitutional regime but, in the end, chose different outcomes.[2] This is done by comparing outcomes from countries that are similar in characteristics underlying the choice of government systems yet operate under different ones. This probability is assessed through a set of variables that are thought to be correlated with the constitutional choice. For example, if constitutional choices are seen to be correlated with geography and if a country was colonised and if so by whom (both used in this literature), then two countries similarly positioned geographically who were colonised by the same country can be thought of having a similar probability of having a presidential regime. If one then does have a presidential regime and the other a parliamentary one, then the difference in outcomes across this pair (or more) of countries can be used for inference. This process is known as propensity score matching.

The second widely used strategy in the face of potential reverse-causality concerns is the use of instrumental variables estimation.[3] In this approach, the potential for reverse causality is mitigated by finding a third variable (different from the constitutional regime of a country and the macroeconomic outcome in question) that is correlated with constitutional choice but is not considered to be a causal driver of the macroeconomic outcome. With this instrument (or a set of instrumental variables), one can proceed in two stages: first, the constitutional choice can be estimated for each country based on this instrumental variable(s); and in the second stage, one can take these estimates for constitutional choice to estimate the impact on macroeconomic outcomes. Importantly, as it is only the *estimates* of the constitutional choice which enter the second stage estimation, and as these are formed on variables which are not considered a causal driver of the macroeconomic variable, the potential for reverse causality is alleviated.[4]

Potential instruments for the constitutional forms in the existing literature can be classified into three broad categories: constitutional timing variables, Hall and Jones instruments on language (the fraction of the population speaking English and the faction speaking other European languages) and latitude, and the colonisation history of the country. PT2003 combine the first two of these, instrumenting for presidential outcomes using the time when the current constitutional form was adopted in the country (using dummy variables for periods before 1920, between 1921 and 1950, between 1951 and 1980, and beyond 1981) and the age of democracy within a given country (measured as the length of time in which the *Polity* database score of a country has been consecutively positive). Added to these are the Hall and Jones language variables representing Western influence in the country and the latitude of the country.

Acemoglu (2005) argues that these make for weak instruments as the constitutional timing variables have limited statistical significance and the main determinants are the Hall and Jones variables which he views as not convincing instruments for constitutional features. Rockey (2012) subsequently extends potential instruments to also include the constitutional history of a country. The argument is that countries are likely to have *inherited* their constitutional features through colonial power; thus, additional variables of whether a country was colonised by the UK, Spain, or another country are included in the set of potential instruments.

Existing political economy literature also provides instruments for institutional quality. For example, Acemoglu *et al.* (2001) present evidence that potential settler mortality is a good instrument for institutional quality as this was correlated with whether colonisers settled in a given colony and subsequently, the quality of the institutions they put in place (which persist to the present day).[5] Likewise, Acemoglu *et al.* (2002) suggest population density in 1500 provides a good instrument for institutional quality. Using similar intuition, Hall and Jones (1999) utilise instruments for language and latitude, as specified earlier. Our approach is to consider a large set of all potential instruments and choose those performing best in diagnostic tests.

We take each of these potential instruments to the data to determine which provides the best fit. Results suggest that a simple specification including a dummy variable for if a country's constitution was established in 1981 or later and if the country was colonised by Spain (both of which are associated with presidential regimes) provides strong instruments for our three variables representing constitutional design (parliamentary versus presidential regimes) with first-stage F-statistics and R^2s of 28.65 and 0.41 for *PTPres*, 45.39 and 0.52 for *PresAll*, and 36.65 and 0.47 for *PresScale*, our three measures of regime choice used in our empirical specifications.[6] A rule-of-thumb for instrumental validity is that the first-stage F-statistic should be above 10, although many argue that this should be above 20 (Staiger and Stock 1997, Stock *et al.* 2002). Importantly, this threshold is reached for all our constitutional variables without the use of the Hall and Jones instruments.

Similar to our approach with constitutional instruments, we explore the performance of these indicators as instruments for our institutional quality variable of choice, the Rule of Law (as used in Rodrik *et al.* 2004), from the Worldwide Governance Indicators of the World Bank (discussed in Chapter 3). We also test the sensitivity of our results to alternative measures of institutional quality. The capped version of settler mortality performs better than the raw measure and both perform significantly better than population density in 1500.[7] The fraction of people speaking English and European languages by themselves are weak instruments but are both statistically significant when included in an estimation with log of settler mortality; however, their inclusion does reduce the value of the first-stage F-test, a key statistic in determining the validity of the instrument. Similar results also hold for the latitude of the country, a measure used by Rodrik *et al.* (2004) in addition to the language variables.

To estimate all the relationships in Figure 1.1 (the casual relationship between constitutional choice and institutional outcomes), we use propensity score matching. To estimate all relationships in Figure 1.1 simultaneously, we follow Rodrik *et al.* (2004) and use a three-stage approach, instrumenting for both constitutional choice and institutional outcomes first and then subsequently estimating their respective impacts on different macroeconomic outcomes. The following system is estimated simultaneously:

$$X_i = \mu + \alpha INS_i + \beta PRES_i + \gamma Z_i + \varepsilon_i$$

$$INS_i = \lambda + \partial SM_i + \varphi GEO_i + \varphi PRES_i + e_i$$

$$PRES_i = \theta + \sigma con81_i + \tau colESP_i + \epsilon_i$$

where X_i is the macroeconomic variable of interest for country i (income, measured through the log of real GDP; inequality, measured through the log of average Gini coefficients; and average inflation), INS_i represents the institutional quality, $PRES_i$ whether a country operates a presidential regime, Z_i a set of control variables, SM_i is capped settler mortality, GEO_i the latitude of a country's capital city, $con81_i$ a dummy variable representing if a constitution was agreed in 1981 or more recent; and $colESP_i$ a dummy variable representing if the country was colonised by Spain.

4.2   The impact of constitutions on institutions: propensity score matching

As an initial test to determine the impact of constitutions on institutions, we use propensity score matching, as discussed in Section 4.1. We follow PT2003 who estimated propensity score for similar variables (including political rents, welfare spending, and the size of government): namely, to estimate the probability of a particular regime, we use the Hall and Jones instruments as well as the log of GDP per capita and *Durable* (discussed earlier) as covariates.[8]

Table 4.1 presents the propensity score matching results for those variables in Table 3.1, comparing the difference between each of the democratic,

Table 4.1 Propensity score matching: democratic, societal, and institutional metrics

Classification	BG2013				PT2003			
	(1) Parl	(2) Pres	(3) Difference	(4) p-Value	(5) Parl	(6) Pres	(7) Difference	(8) p-Value
Panel (a): nature and quality of democracy								
Polity	4.806	1.212	−3.594***	(0.000)	6.541	4.385	−2.156**	(0.016)
ElecDem	0.573	0.457	−0.116**	(0.014)	0.671	0.519	−0.152***	(0.010)
PolStab	0.327	0.006	−0.321*	(0.052)	0.509	0.262	−0.247	(0.452)
Voice	0.547	0.305	−0.242*	(0.076)	0.839	0.347	−0.492**	(0.014)
Panel (b): society								
MediaFree	1.028	0.549	−0.479*	(0.052)	1.296	0.900	−0.396	(0.185)
CivicSoc	0.656	0.563	−0.093***	(0.008)	0.735	0.616	−0.119***	(0.008)
CivilLib	0.733	0.604	−0.129***	(0.000)	0.808	0.661	−0.147***	(0.000)
FreeExp	0.782	0.468	−0.314**	(0.002)	0.854	0.698	−0.156	(0.124)
Panel (c): quality and the inclusiveness of institutions								
GovtEff	0.389	0.155	−0.234	(0.280)	0.908	0.403	−0.505***	(0.001)
RegQual	0.390	0.300	−0.090	(0.655)	0.866	0.504	−0.362***	(0.001)
PartDem	0.376	0.295	−0.081**	(0.021)	0.446	0.337	−0.109**	(0.011)

Note: For each of the variables represented in the first column, the mean for parliamentary regimes from Table 1 is presented (in columns numbered 1 and 5 and presidential regimes in column 2 and 6. Then a propensity score matching test is performed, using Hall and Jones instruments as well as the log of GDP per capita and *Durable*. The estimated differences between the presidential and the parliamentary regimes are presented in columns 3 and 7 with *p*-values from these estimates displayed in columns 4 and 8. As *Durable* is a covariate in the analysis, we do not include it among the institutional variables. A standard star convention is used, with *, **, and *** representing significance levels of 10%, 5%, and 1%, respectively. Both BG2013 and PT2003 are used in classifying presidential versus parliamentary regimes; in the case of the former, semi-presidential systems are not included in the analysis.

societal, and institutional variables, now through propensity score matching. After controlling for potential reverse causality, we observe statistically significant differences in institutional variables across constitutional form: presidential regimes lead to weaker democracies, societies, and institutions. The only exceptions to this are for media freedom (*MediaFree*), political stability (*PolStab*), and freedom of speech (*FreeExp*) for the PT2003 classification of countries and government effectiveness and regulation quality for the BG2013 classification; importantly, in each of these cases, the direction of the estimate is consistent with our results from Chapter 3 (that presidential regimes are associated with weaker values), but these differences are not statistically significant. In all other cases, the results from Chapter 2 are maintained and found to be statistically significant.

Table 4.2 now presents similar results as Table 4.1 for those legislative, electoral, and economic institutions from Table 3.2. For all variables for which there was a statistically significant difference under the two regimes in Table 3.2, this is maintained in Table 4.2. That is, there is evidence that presidential regimes *bring about* weaker legislative power and control, and that they are also associated with lower levels of education, human capital, and trade openness.[9] Taken together, these results present clear evidence that the constitution of a country has a clear impact on its institutions, especially those related to the nature and quality of democracy, society, and legislative power and control.

We have also performed the propensity matching score exercise as presented in Tables 4.1 and 4.2, now dropping the log of GDP as a covariate (as this will be a dependent variable in the next subsection). The results from this exercise are very much in line with those presented in Tables 4.1 and 4.2, revealing quantitatively different but qualitatively robust point estimates.

We also look at these outcomes for semi-presidential regimes (not presented). As the approach requires a binary variable (one with only two outcomes), we do this by iteratively including semi-presidential regimes with presidential regimes (and thus compare this group against parliamentary regimes) and through including semi-presidential countries with parliamentary ones (and thus compare this group with presidential regimes). Similar to that in Chapter 3, we find that semi-presidential outcomes lie in between those of presidential and parliamentary systems; this is evidenced by the fact that results tend to become weaker when including semi-presidential countries, but not overturned. Moreover, we find support that semi-presidential countries behave more like presidential ones than parliamentary ones, as when we compare parliamentary regimes against both presidential and semi-presidential ones, the differences in Tables 4.1 and 4.2 remain (to a large extent) statistically significant.

Table 4.2 Propensity score matching: legislative, electoral, and economic metrics

Classification	BG2013				PT2003			
	(1) Parl	(2) Pres	(3) Difference	(4) p-Value	(5) Parl	(6) Pres	(7) Difference	(8) p-Value
Panel (a): legislative power and control								
RuleOfLaw	0.434	0.052	−0.382	(0.156)	0.855	0.240	−0.615***	(0.007)
Xconst	3.623	1.157	−2.466***	(0.000)	5.484	1.663	−3.821***	(0.000)
PolCon	0.319	0.210	−0.109***	(0.000)	0.367	0.245	−0.122***	(0.000)
JudCon	0.684	0.398	−0.286***	(0.000)	0.776	0.673	−0.103	(0.398)
CorrCon	0.401	0.120	−0.281*	(0.085)	0.845	0.358	−0.487***	(0.006)
Panel (b): electoral system and the number of parties								
Parties	3.945	4.297	0.352	(0.353)	4.084	4.109	0.0248	(0.941)
Majoritarian	0.433	−0.095	−0.528***	(0.000)	0.384	−0.054	−0.438***	(0.000)
Panel (c): economic institutions								
Education	7.584	8.521	0.937	(0.402)	8.069	8.890	0.821***	(0.000)
Openness	86.598	60.588	−26.01*	(0.076)	89.369	95.498	6.129	(0.717)
ExRateVol	121.141	513.540	392.444**	(0.012)	23.523	292.534	269.011	(0.310)
CBI	0.445	0.520	0.0755	(0.130)	0.408	0.533	0.125*	(0.065)
HumanCapital	2.503	2.660	0.157	(0.123)	2.611	2.407	−0.204	(0.103)
Government consumption	19.022	14.774	−4.248*	(0.068)	17.467	15.640	−1.827	(0.457)
Tax revenue	30.435	26.354	−4.081	(0.267)	29.567	28.287	−1.280*	(0.067)
Debt	54.650	52.527	−2.123	(0.875)	54.106	58.931	4.824	(0.768)

Note. Similar to Table 4.1, now analysing differences in *legislative, electoral, and economic institutions* metrics.

4.3 The impact of constitutions and institutions on macroeconomic outcomes

We now look at the impact of both constitutions and institutions on macroeconomic outcomes, simultaneously, and on each other; in this sense, this section tests all channels discussed in Chapter 3. Specification (1) in Table 4.3 presents results simply by estimating the *unconditional* effect of presidential regimes on the log of GDP per capita in 2015; presidential countries are estimated to have statistically significant lower levels of GDP per capita. This reconciles with the findings presented in Chapter 2, with the results suggesting that presidential countries have approximately three times lower GDP per capita.[10]

Specification (2) now controls for the quality of institutions where we observe that although the estimate for the impact of presidential regimes is no longer statistically significant, the sign attached to it has now reversed, with a (much smaller) estimated positive impact of presidential regimes on incomes. Importantly, the quality of institutions is also strongly statistically significant and our estimates in Chapter 3 and earlier in this chapter reveal that presidential regimes have statistically significantly lower quality institutions. Taken together, results from columns (1) and (2) suggest that presidential countries have lower income per person *because of* weaker institutions.

Specification (3) in Table 4.3 is similar to that of specification (1), but with the presidential variable is instrumented as discussed earlier; importantly, the unconditional estimate is still statistically significant and consistent with the result when not instrumented. Specification (4) is similar to that of specification (2) where now both the constitutional and institutional variables are instrumented, where similar results prevail. Institutional quality is positively associated with higher income and, similar to column 2, presidential regimes are estimated to have higher income, importantly, after controlling for instrumental quality. Finally, in specification (5), we drop the settler mortality variable from the instruments to increase the number of observations, again with similar results prevailing.[11]

Specifications (6) and (7) estimate the full model, simultaneously instrumenting for both institutions and constitutions and testing for the importance of presidential regimes on institutions and subsequently both of these on per capita income; the difference between specifications (6) and (7) is that the former includes the settler mortality variable as an instrument for institutions and the latter not, again to expand the sample. The intuition developed throughout the book prevails: presidential countries have a lower quality of institutions, and this result is strongly statistically significant in both specifications. Further, the results from specifications (2), (4), and (5)

Table 4.3 The impact of constitutions and institutions on per capita income

	(1) PTPres	(2) PTPres	(3) PTPres	(4) PTPres	(5) PTPres	(6) PTPres	(7) PTPres	(8) BGPres	(9) BGPres	(10) PresScale	(11) PresScale
Presidential	-1.196*** (0.000)	0.0573 (0.767)	-1.328*** (0.000)	1.551** (0.036)	1.538** (0.033)	1.428** (0.011)	2.777*** (0.000)	1.192** (0.007)	1.943*** (0.000)	1.067*** (0.006)	1.700*** (0.000)
Institutions		1.179*** (0.000)		1.757*** (0.000)	1.934*** (0.000)	1.616*** (0.000)	2.468*** (0.000)	1.572*** (0.000)	2.040*** (0.000)	1.474*** (0.000)	1.870*** (0.000)
SemiPresidential								-0.637 (0.216)	-0.221 (0.346)		
Institutions											
settlermortajr250						-0.258*** (0.004)		-0.213** (0.015)		-0.216** (0.017)	
Latitude						1.478** (0.025)	1.472*** (0.000)	2.347*** (0.002)	2.494*** (0.000)	2.422*** (0.003)	2.493*** (0.000)
Presidential						-0.725** (0.046)	-1.524*** (0.000)	-0.752** (0.021)	-1.123*** (0.000)	-0.713* (0.032)	-1.162*** (0.000)
Presidential											
con81						0.0871 (0.381)	0.325*** (0.000)	0.234** (0.015)	0.250*** (0.000)	0.279*** (0.006)	0.275*** (0.000)
colesp						0.673*** (0.000)	0.566*** (0.000)	0.596*** (0.000)	0.663*** (0.000)	0.578*** (0.000)	0.619*** (0.000)

(Continued)

Table 4.3 (Continued)

	(1) PTPres	(2) PTPres	(3) PTPres	(4) PTPres	(5) PTPres	(6) PTPres	(7) PTPres	(8) BGPres	(9) BGPres	(10) PresScale	(11) PresScale
n	83	82	83	44	82	44	82	42	82	41	81
R-sq	0.191	0.736	0.182	0.394	0.454	0.465	−0.150	0.563	0.306	0.625	0.432
R-sq_2						0.492	0.304	0.476	0.376	0.485	0.373
R-sq_3						0.441	0.395	0.521	0.500	0.514	0.452
Overidentified			0.001	0.263	0.386						

Note. Dependent variable is the log of GDP per capita in 2015; in each specification, a constant is included (not reported). The first row represents the constitutional categorisation variable used: 'PTPres' and 'BGPres' denote presidential regimes as in PT2003 and BG2013, respectively, and 'PresScale' is a variable equal to 0 if BG2013 classify as parliamentary, 0.5 if semi-presidential, and 1 if presidential. For each variable, the point estimate is presented with a *p*-value of its statistical significance in parentheses underneath. A standard star convention is used, with *, **, and *** representing significance levels of 10%, 5%, and 1%, respectively. Robust standard errors are presented throughout. Columns 1 and 3 are based on OLS specifications and columns 2, 4, and 5 on GMM instrumental variable specifications with the instruments of whether a country was colonised by Spain ('colesp') and if the constitutions were written post-1981 ('con81') for constitution and settler mortality and latitude for institutions; in specification (5), we drop settler mortality to increase the number of observations. 'Overidentified' represents *p*-values for overidentification tests; in all cases, there is insufficient evidence to reject the null hypothesis that the overidentifying restrictions are valid. Columns 6–11 are based on a simultaneous equation specification with the log of GDP per capita in 2015 being the dependent variable in the top panel, the quality of institutions in the second panel, and whether a country is presidential in the final panel. Goodness-of-fit is presented for the specifications in the three panels, respectively, by R-sq, R-sq_2, and R-sq_3.

are maintained whereby poor institutional quality leads to lower levels of income, and presidential countries – holding institutional quality constant – are estimated to have higher levels of income. Importantly, factoring the results from the entire specification, presidential countries are typically estimated to have lower levels of income; however, this lower income is *derived from* the poor quality of institutions.[12] That is, presidential countries have lower-quality institutions, and this leads to lower economic income. To frame this around the channels illustrated in Figure 1.1, causality is going through channels B and D, and not directly through A.[13]

Table 4.4 is similar to that of Table 4.3 where now the dependent variable is the average of annual inflation rates for each country since the 1960s. Following MO2018, to remove the influence of outliers, we transform the inflation rate ($\neq$) by using $\pi / (1 + \pi)$ (Cukierman *et al.* 1992).[14] Interestingly, following a similar methodology as earlier, we find that presidential regimes have a consistently unfavourable impact on inflation; that is, holding all else constant, presidential regimes have higher levels of inflation. These results reconcile with those from Chapter 2, with presidential regimes found to exhibit over twice the inflation rate of those parliamentary countries. Moreover, we find that institutional quality does not predict inflation well. Thus, whereas institutional quality fully explains the negative effects of presidential regimes on per capita income, it explains none of the detrimental effects on inflation.

Running the same estimations with a measure of *CBI* among the list of institutions provides similar results as those in Table 4.4; presidential regimes have higher inflation, and, in general, the quality of institutions does not have a statistically significant effect on inflation. Unsurprisingly, an exception to this is the measure of *CBI*, the estimated coefficient of which is statistically significant, suggesting that this specific institution is important for inflation outcomes. Further, note from Chapter 3 that presidential regimes have levels of *CBI* in line with those of parliamentary ones. Thus, the results suggest that central banks have managed to escape the poor quality of other institutions under presidential regimes, but despite this, inflation outcomes are better in countries run by parliamentary systems.

Table 4.5 performs the same analysis as in Tables 4.3 and 4.4 where now income inequality (in the form of the log average Gini coefficient during the years in the 2000s) is the dependent variable. The unconditional estimates [specifications (1) and (3)] suggest that presidential countries have higher levels of income inequality, and this effect is statistically significant. This reconciles with the results from Chapter 2 where presidential regimes are shown to exhibit more than double the Gini coefficient of parliamentary countries. When institutional quality is controlled for [specifications (2) and (4)], however, the estimates on the impact of presidential regimes diminish and,

Table 4.4 The impact of constitutions and institutions on inflation

	(1)	(2)	(3)	(4)	(5)	(6)	(7)	(8)	(9)	(10)	(11)
	PTPres	PTPres	PTPres	PTPres	PTPres	PTPres	PTPres	BGPres	BGPres	BGPresScale	BGPresScale
Presidential	0.0572***	0.0322*	0.111***	0.133***	0.165***	0.132***	0.193***	0.101**	0.121***	0.0992***	0.119***
	(0.001)	(0.069)	(0.000)	(0.001)	(0.003)	(0.004)	(0.000)	(0.011)	(0.000)	(0.010)	(0.000)
Institutions		-0.0249***		0.0110	0.0329	-0.00623	0.0430**	-0.0124	0.00333	-0.0146	0.00215
		(0.006)		(0.522)	(0.135)	(0.762)	(0.031)	(0.456)	(0.791)	(0.369)	(0.845)
Semi-Pres								-0.0337	0.0162		
								(0.511)	(0.404)		
Institutions											
Settler mortality						-0.214**		-0.168		-0.163	
						(0.048)		(0.104)		(0.115)	
Latitude						2.216***	1.845***	3.347***	3.072***	3.500***	2.960***
						(0.004)	(0.000)	(0.000)	(0.000)	(0.000)	(0.000)
Presidential						-0.775*	-1.398***	-0.668**	-0.885***	-0.644*	-0.998***
						(0.052)	(0.000)	(0.048)	(0.005)	(0.063)	(0.001)
Presidential											
con81						0.107	0.326***	0.220**	0.258***	0.254***	0.291***
						(0.266)	(0.000)	(0.017)	(0.000)	(0.008)	(0.000)
colesp						0.654***	0.594***	0.622***	0.672***	0.607***	0.614***
						(0.000)	(0.000)	(0.000)	(0.000)	(0.000)	(0.000)
n	82	81	82	43	81	43	81	41	80	40	79
R-sq	0.155	0.265	0.015	0.110	0.071	0.098	-0.754	0.226	0.016	0.248	0.066
R-sq_2						0.513	0.363	0.521	0.437	0.527	0.432
R-sq_3						0.441	0.399	0.525	0.490	0.522	0.442
Overidentified			0.543	0.577	0.280						

Note. Dependent variable is the average of transformed inflation $(\neq)$ by using $\pi / (1 + \pi)$ – calculated over the period from 1960 up to the end of each sample period. As inflation represents rates of change and not levels, unlike the level of income (Table 4.3) and the level of inequality (Table 4.4), we look at the average over the period for the majority of our data. All other notation and specification choices are as earlier.

Table 4.5 The impact of constitutions and institutions on income inequality

	(1) PTPres	(2) PTPres	(3) PTPres	(4) PTPres	(5) PTPres	(6) PTPres	(7) PTPres	(8) BGPres	(9) BGPres	(10) BGPresScale	(11) BGPresScale
Presidential	0.253*** (0.000)	0.141*** (0.004)	0.407*** (0.000)	0.141 (0.135)	0.0965 (0.509)	0.0727 (0.523)	-0.00413 (0.977)	0.175** (0.033)	0.114 (0.185)	0.172** (0.043)	0.0782 (0.390)
Institutions		-0.0992*** (0.000)		-0.110** (0.010)	-0.188*** (0.007)	-0.159*** (0.002)	-0.259*** (0.000)	-0.109** (0.003)	-0.173*** (0.000)	-0.111** (0.003)	-0.196*** (0.000)
Semi-Pres									-0.0887 (0.055)		
Institutions											
Settler mortality						-0.219** (0.029)		-0.256*** (0.008)		-0.259*** (0.007)	
Latitude						2.246*** (0.001)	2.672*** (0.000)	2.702*** (0.001)	3.485*** (0.000)	2.782*** (0.001)	3.375*** (0.000)
Presidential						-0.881** (0.028)	-1.065*** (0.002)	-0.678** (0.035)	-0.795*** (0.009)	-0.684** (0.043)	-0.953*** (0.002)
Presidential											
con81						0.158* (0.095)	0.235*** (0.002)	0.216** (0.023)	0.233*** (0.000)	0.236** (0.015)	0.241*** (0.000)
colesp						0.638*** (0.000)	0.658*** (0.000)	0.613*** (0.000)	0.703*** (0.000)	0.601*** (0.000)	0.650*** (0.000)
n	79	78	79	42	78	42	78	40	80	39	79
R-sq	0.292	0.419	0.182	0.293	0.298	0.178	0.082	0.439	0.490	0.405	0.370
R-sq_2						0.534	0.389	0.543	0.444	0.545	0.441
R-sq_3						0.444	0.436	0.530	0.519	0.528	0.474
Overidentified			0.294	0.358	0.003						

Note: Dependent variable is the log of the average Gini coefficient throughout the 2000s; Gini coefficients are not available for each country for each year; thus, we take these averages to represent the general level of inequality. All other notation and specification choices are as in Table 4.3.

in specification (4), become statistically insignificant. This is consistent with the intuition developed in Chapter 3 and earlier in Section 4.2 of this chapter. That is, presidential regimes feature lower institutional quality, and lower institutional quality leads to higher income inequality. Thus, when the specifications control for institutional quality, the estimated impact of presidential regimes diminishes; that, is, some of the variation being picked in the unconditional estimates is from the variation of institutional quality across the two forms of government.

When the full system of equations is estimated [specifications (6)–(11)], it is observed that most of the variation is coming through the institutional channel. That is, presidential regimes are estimated to have statistically significantly lower levels of institutional quality and lower levels of institutional quality lead to higher income inequality. In two specifications (8) and (10), even after controlling for this relationship, there is a statistically significant increase in income inequality for presidential regimes, holding institutional quality constant; however, the consistent message in Table 4.5 is that much of the impact of constitutions on inequality is through their impacts on institutions.

4.4 Robustness

In addition to the sensitivity tests outlined earlier, we have performed a number of additional robustness checks to test the sensitivity of our findings to varying empirical specifications, estimation methods, and alternative instruments. For brevity, only the presidential variable from PT2003 is used in specifications (1)–(5) in Tables 4.3–4.5; performing the same analysis with BG2013 classification, either as dummies or in its 'scale' version provides results in line with those earlier. Further, the instrumental variable estimation used in producing the results in Tables 4.3–4.5 is based on the generalised method of moments; using limited-information maximum likelihood or two-stage least squares also provides similar results.

Tables 4.3–4.5 include two (moderately) different specifications for instrumental variables for both constitutional and institutional variables. As a sensitivity check, we follow the approach of MO2018 and PT2003 in including the Hall and Jones language and trade variables and all constitutional timing dummy variables as instrumental variables.[15] Note we do not do this in our original specification for three reasons: first, issues related to the excludability of these instruments (Acemoglu 2005, discussed in Section 4.1); second, the goodness of fit of these instruments relative to the alternatives; and, third, the need to keep the specifications as small as possible given the low number of observations. Importantly, results from these specifications are in line with those from Tables 4.3–4.5, with presidential countries having lower income and higher inequality through the impact of their constitution and institutions, and presidential countries having higher levels of inflation, independent of institutions.

Moreover, Tables 4.3–4.5 use the *RuleOfLaw* to proxy for general institutional quality; we further extend this to include constraints on the chief executive (*Xconst*), legislative control (*PolCon*), government effectiveness (*GovtEff*), and *Polity*; the results from earlier are robust to these different specifications. Importantly, there is little evidence from any of these institutional variables that they influence average rates of inflation.

4.5 Discussion and Conclusions

The results from our specifications are illustrated in Figure 4.1 which has three panels for the three dependent variables earlier. On each of the *x*-axis is the rule of law (our benchmark measure of institutional quality) and on the *y*-axis are the three dependent variables (in the three separate panels). Each observation is a point in the figure, with presidential countries labelled with a dot and parliamentary ones with an asterisk. In each panel, lines of best fit are presented for both presidential (solid line) and parliamentary (dashed line) countries. Finally, the vertical and horizontal lines represent the mean values for each variable across all countries. Importantly, all data in these figures are observational and do not instrument out either regime choice or institutional quality (unlike the main specifications in Tables 4.3–4.5).

For example, panel (a) of Figure 4.1 presents results for the log of GDP in 2015; here one can see that those countries with weaker rule of law tend to have a lower level of income (there is a very clear correlation) and this is true for both parliamentary and presidential countries. Further, 60% of all presidential countries sit in the bottom-left (those with both below-average rule of law and income per capita); 79% below-average rule of law, whereas 49% of all parliamentary countries sit in the top-right quadrant (above-average institutions and income); however, what is also illustrated in panel (a) of Figure 4.1 is that if presidential countries can have better institutions, they can at least have the same level of income and possibly even better. This reconciles with the results from Table 4.3.

From panel (b) of Figure 4.1, presidential countries have significantly higher levels of average inflation, and even after controlling for institutional quality, these outcomes are worse; these results reconcile to Table 4.4. Finally, panel (c) of Figure 4.1 present results which suggest that once controlling for institutions, presidential countries have similar outcomes with respect to income inequality, but that they have weaker institutions (reconciling with the results from Table 4.5).

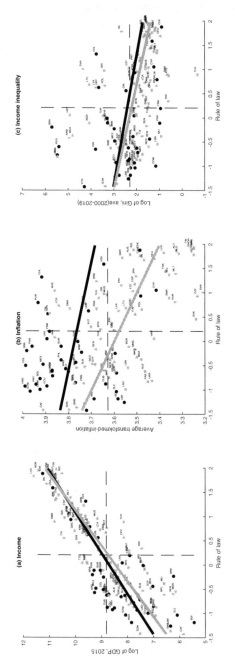

Figure 4.1 Rule of law and macroeconomic outcomes.

This chapter has combined different components of the linkages between government systems and economic outcomes, previously developed in multiple stages; direct effects of government form on economic outcomes and indirect effects working through the institutions. Chapter 2 has already established that presidential regimes produce inferior economic outcomes relative to parliamentary regimes across a wide range of metrics, including widely used economic performance measures such as per capita income and inflation rate as well as human development measures such as life expectancy. Chapter 3 has documented that institutions vary under the two government systems, with those under presidential regimes exhibiting less favourable attributes.

Combining the two sets of relationships, Chapter 4 has adopted an empirical strategy incorporating the possibility of both direct and indirect – through the role of varying institutions – role of government systems on economic outcomes and empirically established both sets of effects. For example, we found that while government systems only affect income levels indirectly – through the role of institutions – direct effects are important in the determination of income inequality. Interestingly, variations in the institutions are found to have no role in determining inflationary outcomes that are significantly worse in presidential regimes.

These findings in turn offer important policy implications. For example, our estimates from per capita income regressions reveal that presidential regimes would have also achieved better income levels if they chose better institutions, and hence it is the institutions, not the form of government, that determine the per capita income levels. Improving institutional quality is also associated with more equal income distribution, although there is also a direct impact of the regime choice on distributional outcomes.

Notes

1 Existing empirical evidence suggests that when changes in form of government take place, these changes are influenced more by political factors such as the characteristics of the political system, political leaders, and political conflict and not economic or sociodemographic factors (see, for example, Hayo and Voigt 2010).
2 See, for example, Caliendo *et al.* (2008) and Thoemmes and Kim (2011).
3 See, for example, Sargan (1958), Newey (1990), Hansen *et al.* (2008), and Sovey and Green (2011).
4 Also see PT2003, Chapter 5 for a comprehensive review of both the propensity score matching and the instrumental variables estimation techniques, and importantly within the context of analysing constitutions and their economic effects.
5 This is extended in Acemoglu *et al.* (2002) to cap settler mortality for those outliers with higher levels (250 annualised deaths per year).

6 'PTPres' and 'BGPres' denote presidential regimes as in PT2003 and BG2013, respectively, and 'PresScale' is a variable equal to 0 if BG2013 classify as parliamentary, 0.5 if semi-presidential, and 1 if presidential.

7 There are first stage F-tests of 45.35, 72.01, and 1.59 for settler mortality, settler mortality capped, and population density, respectively. A similar ranking of first stage F-tests results when also including Hall and Jones (1999) language variables (23.52, 35.52, and 18.36, respectively).

8 The exception to this is when in the resulting specification, the treatment overlap assumption has been violated and thus the test does not converge, and in such a case, we remove (where possible) one covariate to keep the estimates as consistent as possible. If the overlap assumption is violated, it represents cases where there is limited overlap (or similarity) between the two groups in the data (the treatment and control, in our case, presidential and parliamentary countries).

9 There is less evidence that parliamentary countries having either higher levels of government consumption or tax revenue, with these differences only being slightly significant and for only one classification of regime.

10 This is calculated by using the exponential of the point estimate of 1.243.

11 The bottom of Table 4.3 provides p-values for overidentification tests; there is insufficient evidence to reject the null hypothesis that the overidentifying restrictions are valid for specifications (4) and (5). Thus, in combination with the results in Section 4.1, there is evidence that the instruments are relevant and valid. This is not true for specification (3); however, we present this only for exposition purposes.

12 Formally, this is calculated as the coefficient estimate on impact of constitutions on institutions [−0.751 in specification (6)] multiplied by the estimate for the impact of institutional quality on income (1.428) plus the estimate of the impact of presidential regimes on income, holding all else constant (1.428). In the larger specifications (7), (9), and (11), the results from this exercise are large and negative; in specifications (8) and (10), these are very close to zero, and in specification (6), this is a slight positive.

13 Note for specification (7) a negative R-squared is reported. This technically comes from estimating a structural model whilst using instrumental variables. This allows for the possibility that the residual sum of squares from the structural model is greater than the total sum of squares from the data. Importantly, it does not invalidate the parameter estimates that are consistent with the narrative being developed in specifications (1)–(6). Further, this issue does not arise with the R-squared's in later estimations (which importantly have more observations), allowing us to make inference based on all the results in the table.

14 We have tested the sensitivity of our results to using the untransformed rates of inflation, and these provide results in line with those with this transformed version.

15 For the simultaneous equation specification, we do not include the Hall and Jones variables which Acemoglu (2005) classifies as 'excludable'.

References

Acemoglu, D. (2005) 'Constitutions, politics, and economics: A review essay on Persson and Tabellini's The economic effects of constitutions', *Journal of Economic Literature*, 43, 1025–1048.

Acemoglu, D., Johnson, S. and Robinson, J.A. (2001) 'The colonial origins of comparative development: An empirical investigation', *American Economic Review*, 91(5), 1369–1401.

Acemoglu, D., Johnson, S. and Robinson, J.A. (2002) 'Reversal of fortune: Geography and institutions in the making of the modern world income distribution', *The Quarterly Journal of Economics*, 117(4), 1231–1294.

Caliendo, M. and Kopeinig, S. (2008) 'Some practical guidance for the implementation of propensity score matching', *Journal of Economic Surveys*, 22(1), 31–72.

Cukierman, A., Web, S. and Neyapti, B. (1992) 'Measuring the independence of central banks and its effect on policy outcomes', *World Bank Economic Review*, 6(3), 353–398.

Hall, R.E. and Jones, C.I. (1999) 'Why do some countries produce so much more output per worker than others?', *The Quarterly Journal of Economics*, 114(1), 83–116.

Hansen, C., Hausman, J. and Newey, W. (2008) 'Estimation with many instrumental variables', *Journal of Business & Economic Statistics*, 26(4), 398–422.

Hayo, B. and Voigt, S. (2010) 'Determinants of constitutional change: Why do countries change their form of government?', *Journal of Comparative Economics*, 38(3), 283–305.

Newey, W.K. (1990) 'Efficient instrumental variables estimation of nonlinear models', *Econometrica*, 809–837.

Rockey, J. (2012) 'Reconsidering the fiscal effects of constitutions', *European Journal of Political Economy*, 28(3), 313–323.

Rodrik, D., Subramanian, A. and Trebbi, F. (2004) 'Institutions rule: The primacy of institutions over geography and integration in economic development', *Journal of Economic Growth*, 9(2), 131–165.

Sargan, J.D. (1958) 'The estimation of economic relationships using instrumental variables', *Econometrica*, 393–415.

Sovey, A.J. and Green, D.P. (2011) 'Instrumental variables estimation in political science: A readers' guide', *American Journal of Political Science*, 55(1), 188–200.

Staiger, D. and Stock, J.H. (1997) 'Instrumental variables regression with weak instruments', *Econometrica*, 65(3), 557–586.

Stock, J.H., Wright, J.H. and Yogo, M. (2002) 'A survey of weak instruments and weak identification in generalized method of moments', *Journal of Business & Economic Statistics*, 20(4), 518–529.

Thoemmes, F.J. and Kim, E.S. (2011) 'A systematic review of propensity score methods in the social sciences', *Multivariate Behavioral Research*, 46(1), 90–118.

5 Discussion and conclusions

The main purpose of this book has been to provide a systematic analysis of the linkages between constitutional form and economic outcomes. As is set out in Chapter 1, the source of our motivation for doing so has been twofold. First, while existing work has made significant progress in establishing the economic effects of constitutions, the mechanism through which constitutional form impacts economic outcomes is still largely unknown. Second, the recent retreat in democracy and the underlying deterioration in democratic institutions highlight the importance of a better understanding of institutions' role in economic outcomes. Importantly, the move towards less democracy, more populism, and authoritarianism has been observed in both presidential and parliamentary regimes and in advanced as well as emerging economies, providing significant scope for identifying the economic consequences of both constitutional rules and institutions.

5.1 Summary

To investigate the impact of government form on economic outcomes by fully incorporating the role of institutions, we built our argument in three stages. We first established the link between government systems and institutions. The key question in this part of the analysis was whether institutions under presidential regimes were systematically different from those under parliamentary ones. In answering this question, we have used an extensive set of institutional variables in testing whether institutions vary across the two government systems and presented significant evidence, both formally and informally, that they do. In the second stage, we analysed the effect of institutions and constitutions on economic outcomes by utilizing a range of institutional variables and a number of economic performance indicators. Finally, we jointly estimated the role of government systems in economic performance while also explicitly incorporating for the link between

DOI: 10.4324/9781003141242-5

governance and institutions on the one hand and the between institutions and economic outcomes on the other.

Separate from our formal empirical analysis, we revisited existing work on the economic effects of constitutions. In Chapter 2, by utilizing data from 138 countries over the period 1960–2019, we observed a clear role for government systems in human development and economic performance. For example, we showed that presidential regimes are consistently associated with inferior human development outcomes such as lower life expectancy, higher infant mortality, and food insecurity. We have also reaffirmed that presidential regimes do worse on economic performance, consistently exhibiting lower growth rates of per capita income, higher inflation, and greater income inequality relative to parliamentary ones.

In Chapter 3, we analysed the linkages between constitutional form and political, legal, and economic institutions. We have utilised a rich dataset on a variety of institutional variables in each category measuring the quality of democracy, inclusiveness of institutions, ideological polarisation, separation of power, rule of law, civil liberties, freedom of speech and media freedoms, education, human capital, and quality of economic policy-making institutions. Our analysis in Chapter 3 established an unambiguous link between government systems and institutional quality. We found that parliamentary regimes featured superior institutions in the form of longer periods of democratic stability, greater democratic participation and democratic agency, greater media freedoms and civil liberties, as well as greater checks and balances in the form of judicial controls on the executive. Furthermore, parliamentary systems are shown to be associated with more favourable economic infrastructure exemplified by better corruption control, better schooling and human capital accumulation, greater openness to trade, and lower exchange rate volatility.

Chapter 4 presented our formal empirical estimation combining the first and second stages of our analysis by exploring (*i*) how government systems influence institutions and (*ii*) how institutions and government systems simultaneously influence economic outcomes. As such, Chapter 4 looked at the economic effects of both constitutions and institutions while explicitly incorporating the association between the two. Interestingly, we have found that much of the variation in economic outcomes can be explained by the variation in the type and the quality of institutions. To the extent that constitutions are a major driver of institutions, a key mechanism through which constitutions influence economic outcomes appears to operate through their role in the making of those institutions. For example, institutions are the main drivers of the per capita income growth, and the reason why this is lower under presidential than under parliamentary systems is found to be due to the poor quality of institutions under the former relative to the latter.

Indeed, there was evidence to suggest that should a presidential country manage to develop strong institutions, the fact that they run a presidential regime may *improve* income per person. Regarding income inequality outcomes, while much of the variation in income inequality comes from variation in institutional quality, presidential regimes exhibit worse income inequality independently from the role of institutions. Different from these two cases, we also found that institutional quality is not a good predictor of inflationary outcomes and the direct effect of government systems on inflation is strong. This is also consistent with the observation that inflationary performance under presidential regimes has been distinctly worse than that under the parliamentary ones throughout our sample period.

5.2 What have we learned?

As we discussed in Chapter 1, the substantial body of existing work on the functioning and consequences of presidential versus parliamentary regimes highlights two important aspects of presidentialism: (*i*) presidents are too powerful, leading to worse outcomes (the *perils of presidentialism*, Linz 1990), but (*ii*) presidents can be decisive, with potentially favourable implications (Ellis and Samuel 2009). These two arguments do not need to be mutually exclusive and both can be true; indeed, Shugart and Carey (1992) argued that it was not the presidentialism *per se* but the power of the executive that was at the source of democratic instability under presidential regimes. That is, typically presidential regimes are bad, but, if one is able to install inclusive institutions, this effect can be mitigated and even outweighed as we have shown in the case of economic growth outcomes. Our findings revealed that the combination of strong institutions and a president *can* be good for income, yet *in practice,* these regimes commonly feature worse institutions and hence are associated with worse outcomes.

This also reconciles with our results on income inequality; although presidential regimes are estimated to have more inequality than parliamentary countries, much of the statistical difference was observed as operating through institutions. This is consistent with both that: presidential regimes are less conducive to stable democracy (Linz 1990) and democratic consolidation is stronger under parliamentarism relative to that under presidentialism, leading to greater democratic stability under the former relative to the latter (Mainwaring 1990, Shugart and Carey 1992, Linz 1994, Stepan and Skach 1993, Cheibub *et al.* 2004), and that the decisiveness of the executive and hence a strong president can be beneficial in unifying political factions (Ellis and Samuel 2009). Importantly, these theories are not mutually.

Our results reveal that on average presidential countries have higher income inequality, but that were presidential countries to have more inclusive institutions; they would have *similar* income inequality outcomes.

How does this reconcile with our results which find that inflation is higher in presidential countries independent of institutions and that institutions (except for *CBI*) have a limited impact on average inflation? An important determinant in controlling inflation is consistent, credible policy driving low inflation expectations. The assertiveness of a president and the lack of democratic consolidation could be seen to lead to less consistency and credibility of the policy. This would be especially acute when inflation is rising, which is seen to be the periods during which presidential countries have higher inflation compared to parliamentary ones in Figure 2.3.

One can draw two lessons from our findings. The first and key contribution of our work is the role of institutions in intermediating the form of government's influence on economic outcomes. As such, our work here has provided one potential explanation for why presidential regimes are bad for the economy. Our findings suggest that the answer to this question lies in the significantly inferior quality of institutions under presidential regimes, which bring about significantly inferior economic outcomes. Indeed, presidential regimes typically operate in weaker democracies lacking proper checks and balances where strong executives (a common aspect of presidentialism) are more likely to bear harmful effects. That is, a good democracy is needed for presidential systems to function well, a point also noted by PT2003. It therefore follows that the question of institutional infrastructure within which government systems operate may be more important than the individual regime itself. Put differently, the appropriate design of a presidential or a parliamentary system may be more important than the choice between the two.

The second lesson one can draw from our findings is related to the retreat in the democratic nature of regimes across the globe over the last two decades, as discussed in Chapter 1. Our findings on the importance of institutions in general, and on the role of the nature and the quality of democracy in particular, as key determinants of economic outcomes suggest that the cost of such democratic regress goes beyond their implications on political stability and is likely to be much more extensive than commonly acknowledged. One recent example of how democratic regimes are better able to design and execute better economic policy is provided by the COVID-19 episode. Countries with better quality and more inclusive democratic institutions have provided significantly larger and more inclusive policy packages in response to the pandemic than countries lacking these institutions.

5.3 Suggestions for future work

While we believe that our work in this book will help bridge the gap between existing research in economics and political science on the consequences of constitutional rules, there is still a long way to go. Our framework entailed two phases in constitutions' impact on economic outcomes: (*i*) government systems influencing institutions – mostly the interest of political scientists since the 19th century and (*ii*) institutions shaping economic outcomes – the core focus of institutional economics research since the early 1990s. Our empirical analysis has combined these two lines of argument while also retaining the direct impact of government systems on economic performance.

Based on a rich set of political, legal, and economic institutions, our findings have provided strong support for the hypothesis that presidential regimes consistently feature weaker institutions. We have also established that strong institutions are associated with superior economic outcomes, forming a clear linkage between government systems and economic performance. In establishing this link, we have focussed on the role of constitutional rules in the making of institutions and the role of institutions in outcomes. An important aspect of this relationship, which we have excluded here, is how constitutions and hence institutions shape policy itself. For example, while we observed significant differences in inflationary performance under the presidential versus parliamentary system, our work is silent on what differences in economic policy have contributed to such outcomes. For example, are presidential regimes more likely than parliamentary ones to be associated with certain types of economic policies? Unsurprisingly, much of the existing work on differentiating between the effects of government systems since PT2003 focuses on fiscal policy. This is natural given that fiscal policy is the obvious domain over which the influence of government types – whether in political ideology or in governance system – is expected to be felt. After all, treasury departments almost always function as parts of government as opposed to other arms of economic policy such as central banks that are typically independent of political authority even in less developed economies though to a lesser extent. Nonetheless, it is still possible that even policies that are under the direct control of the government may behave differently under the two systems of government. Clearly, economic outcomes are likely to be shaped by a combination of economic policies, including monetary and fiscal policy actions.

Among the recent additions to these two arms of policy is unconventional monetary policy – large-scale asset purchases, liquidity support, and central bank swap operations – and macroprudential policy consisting of countercyclical capital and borrowing requirements aimed at ensuring financial stability. Both these new sets of policies became an integral part of the policy toolbox in the wake of the global financial crisis in 2008–2009, especially in advanced economies. Emerging economies had already started implementing macroprudential policy in the 1990s following their own crisis experiences.

A substantial body of work on the effects of a macroprudential policy that has emerged in the last two decades clearly establishes the impact of these new policy tools on equilibrium outcomes. Potential distributional implications of both unconventional monetary and macroprudential policies have also been widely debated in both academic and policy circles.

There is also the recent expansion of the tools at the disposal of policy-makers, with the addition of climate action instruments such as climate-friendly tax and spending, carbon pricing, green bonds, and financial policy prioritising green investment. While it is still early days in the implementation of climate policy, a large and increasing number of countries are now adopting a wealth of policy tools against climate change, a movement significantly speeded up by the global pandemic. This trend will allow the fast accumulation of data on the use and effects of climate policy tools. A systematic analysis of whether such policies – as well as those of unconventional and macroprudential ones – differ under different government systems as and when data become available is likely to provide vital new insights into the differential economic effects of the two forms of government.

References

Cheibub, J.A., Przeworski, A. and Saiegh, S.M. (2004) 'Government coalitions and legislative success under presidentialism and parliamentarism', *British Journal of Political Science*, 34(4), 565–587.

Ellis, A. and Samuels, K. (2009) *Making Presidentialism Work: Sharing and Learning from Global Experience*. Cómo Hacer Que Funcione el Sistema Presidencial (Making Presidentialism Work). México, DF: Universidad Nacional Autónoma de México-Instituto de Investigaciones Jurídicas.

Linz, J. (1990) 'The perils of presidentialism', *Journal of Democracy*, 1(1), 51–69.

Linz, J. (1994) 'Presidential or parliamentary democracy: Does it make a difference?', in J.J. Linz and A. Valenzuela (eds.), *The Failure of Presidential Democracy*. Baltimore: John Hopkins University Press, pp. 3–87.

Mainwaring, S. (1990) 'Presidentialism in Latin America', *Latin American Research Review*, 25(1), 157–179.

Shugart, M.S. and Carey, J. (1992) *Presidents and Assemblies: Constitutional Design and Electoral Dynamics*. Cambridge: Cambridge University Press.

Stepan, A. and Skach, C. (1993) 'Constitutional frameworks and democratic consolidation: Parliamentarianism versus presidentialism', *World Politics*, 46(1), 1–22.

Appendix

Table A2.1 Data appendix

Variable	Source and Description
	Macroeconomic outcomes
GDP per capita	GDP per capita (constant 2010 US$), obtained from the World Bank
Gini coefficients	Gini coefficients, obtained from the World Income Inequality Database
Inflation	Percentage change in consumer prices, data obtained from the World Bank
	Constitutions
PTPres	A binary measure indicating if a country is operating under a presidential regime; data obtained from Persson and Tabellini (2003). A country is defined to be presidential if the elected assembly cannot remove the head of state.
BGPres	A binary measure indicating if a country is operating under a presidential regime; data obtained from Bormann and Golder (2013). A country is deemed to have a presidential regime where the government is not responsible to the legislative assembly, and as such cannot be removed by this elected assembly.
Semi-pres	A binary measure indicating if a country is operating under a semi-presidential regime; data obtained from Bormann and Golder (2013). A country is deemed to have a semi-presidential regime where a popularly elected president with a fixed term can be removed by the assembly.
PresScale	A variable equal to one if BGPres equals one, equal to 0.5 if Semi-pres is equal to one, and zero otherwise.
Maj	A binary measure indicating if a country is operating under a majoritarian voting system; data obtained from Bormann and Golder (2013).

Variable	Source and Description
NumParties	Effective number of electoral parties in an election where an average is taken over the course of the panel; data obtained from Bormann and Golder (2013).

Democracy

Variable	Source and Description
Polity	Measure of democracy within a given country on a (−10,10) scale; higher values relating to higher degrees of democracy and lower values indicating greater degrees of autocracy. Data obtained from the Polity IV Project.
Durable	The length of time for which a country has had a continuously positive Polity score.
ElecDem	A measure of the level to which the ideal of electoral democracy is achieved; data obtained from the Varieties of Democracy database.
PolStab	Variable measuring agents' perceptions of the likelihood of political instability and/or politically-motivated violence, including terrorism.
Voice	Variable measuring agents perceived confidence in the voice and accountability of a country, in particular, if citizens are able to participate in selecting their government, as well as freedom of expression, freedom of association, and a free media; data obtained from the Worldwide Governance Indicators.

Society

Variable	Source and Description
MediaFree	The degree to which media is free from government; data obtained from the Varieties of Democracy database.
CivicSoc	A measure of society participation through the degree to which policymakers consult society; data obtained from the Varieties of Democracy database.
CivilLib	A measure of the degree to which civil liberties are respected in a country; data obtained from Varieties of Democracy database.
FreeExp	A variable measuring media and press freedoms; data obtained from the Varieties of Democracy database.

Institutions

Variable	Source and Description
GovtEff	Variable measuring agents' perceptions of government effectiveness, both with respect to the quality of public services and expenditures (including government employees) and the degree to which these are credible and free from political pressures; data obtained from the Worldwide Governance Indicators.

(*Continued*)

Table A2.1 (Continued)

Variable	Source and Description
RegQual	Variable measuring agents' perceptions of regulatory quality, with respect to both the formation and implementation of policies that promote private sector development; data obtained from the Worldwide Governance Indicators.
PartDem	A measure of the level to which democracy is participatory within a country; data obtained from the Varieties of Democracy database.

Power and control

RuleOfLaw	Variable measuring agents perceived confidence in the rule of law of a country, in particular over contract enforcement, property rights, the police, and the courts; data obtained from the Worldwide Governance Indicators.
Xconst	Measure of constraints on chief executive where lower numbers represent fewer constraint; data obtained from the Polity IV Project.
PolCon	Measure of the feasibility of change in policy given the structure of a nation's political institutions and the preference of the actors that inhabit them; data obtained from the POLCON database (https://mgmt.wharton.upenn.edu/faculty/heniszpolcon/polcondataset/).
JudCon	A measure of judicial constraints on the government, the extent to which the executive complies with court rulings, and the judiciary is able to act independently of the government; data obtained from the Varieties of Democracy database.
CorrCon	Variable measuring agents' perceptions of corruption control; data obtained from the Worldwide Governance Indicators.

Economic

Education	Metric of education measured as the average total number of years of education; data obtained from Barro and Lee (2013).
Openness	The sum of imports and exports expressed as a fraction of GDP; data obtained from the World Bank.
ExRateVol	Standard deviation of the exchange rate expressed as a fraction against the US dollar over the sample period; data obtained from Penn World Tables.
CBI	Measure of central bank independence obtained from Cukierman *et al.* (1992), Polillo and Guillén. (2005), Crowe and Meade (2008), all of whom use the same methodology.
HumanCapital	Index of human capital per person, based on years of schooling and returns to education; data obtained from the Penn World Table.

Variable	Source and Description
Government consumption	General government final consumption expenditure to GDP, obtained from the World Bank.
Tax revenue	Tax revenue to GDP, obtained from the World Bank.
Debt	Central government debt to GDP, obtained from the World Bank.

Fertility	
Fertility	Fertility rate, total (births per woman), obtained from the World Bank.
MaternalMortality	Maternal mortality ratio (national estimate, per 100,000 live births), obtained from the World Bank.
LowBirthWeight	Low-birthweight babies (% of births), obtained from the World Bank.
Infant mortality	Mortality rate, infant (per 1,000 live births), obtained from the World Bank.
AdolescentFertility	Adolescent fertility rate (births per 1,000 women ages 15–19), obtained from the World Bank.

Life expectancy	
LifeExpectancy	Life expectancy at birth, total (years), obtained from the World Bank.
LifeExpectancy Female	Life expectancy at birth, female (years), obtained from the World Bank.
LifeExpectancy Male	Life expectancy at birth, male (years), obtained from the World Bank.

Other health and well-being	
FoodInsecurity	Prevalence of severe food insecurity in the population (%), obtained from the World Bank.
Happiness	Response to question 'Taking all things together, would you say you are' from the joint European Values Survey and World Values Survey, 2017–2020 wave.
COVIDDeaths	Deaths – cumulative total per 100,000 population, obtained from the World Health Organisation (4 February 2022).

Instruments	
Settler mortality	Potential settler mortality of colonising powers, obtained from Acemoglu *et al.* (2001).
Latitude	The geographical latitude of a country.
Colonisation	Binary variables determining if the country was colonised by the United Kingdom, Spain, or another country (three separate dummy variables); data obtained from Persson and Tabellini (2003).

Table A4.1 Countries in our dataset by constitutional classification

	BG2013 Classification			
	Parliamentary	Semi-Presidential	Presidential	Not in Dataset
Parliamentary	Australia, Belgium, Bangladesh, The Bahamas, Belize, Barbados, Canada, Czech Republic, Germany, Denmark, Spain, Estonia, Fiji, United Kingdom, Greece, Hungary, India, Israel, Italy, Jamaica, Japan, Luxembourg, Latvia, Malta, Mauritius, Netherlands, Norway, Nepal, New Zealand, Papua New Guinea, Sweden, Thailand, Trinidad and Tobago, Turkey, St. Vincent and the Grenadines	Austria, Bulgaria, Finland, France, Ireland, Iceland, Poland, Portugal, Romania, Senegal, Slovak Republic, Taiwan, Ukraine		Botswana, Malaysia, Singapore, South Africa
President	Pakistan		Argentina, Bolivia, Brazil, Switzerland, Chile, Colombia, Costa Rica, Cyprus, Dominican Republic, Ecuador, Ghana, Guatemala, Honduras, Korea Republic, Mexico, Malawi, Nicaragua, Peru, Philippines, Paraguay, El Salvador, Sri Lanka, Uruguay, United States, Venezuela	Belarus, The Gambia, Namibia, Russian Federation, Uganda, Zambia, Zimbabwe

PT2003 classification

BG2013 Classification

	Parliamentary	Semi-Presidential	Presidential	Not in Dataset
Not in dataset	Andorra, Albania, Antigua and Barbuda, Bhutan, Czechoslovakia, Dominica, Grenada, Kiribati, St. Kitts and Nevis, Lao PDR, Lebanon, St. Lucia, Liechtenstein, Moldova, Marshall Islands, Sudan, Solomon Islands, San Marino, Slovenia, Tuvalu, Vanuatu	Armenia, Central African Republic, Cabo Verde, Congo, Rep., Croatia, Georgia, Guinea-Bissau, Lithuania, Madagascar, Macedonia (FYR), Mali, Mongolia, Mauritania, Niger, Serbia, Sao Tome and Principe, Timor-Leste, Kyrgyzstan	Burundi, Benin, Comoros, Cuba, Micronesia, Indonesia, Kenya, Liberia, Maldives, Nigeria, Panama, Palau, Suriname, Sierra Leone	

PT2003 classification

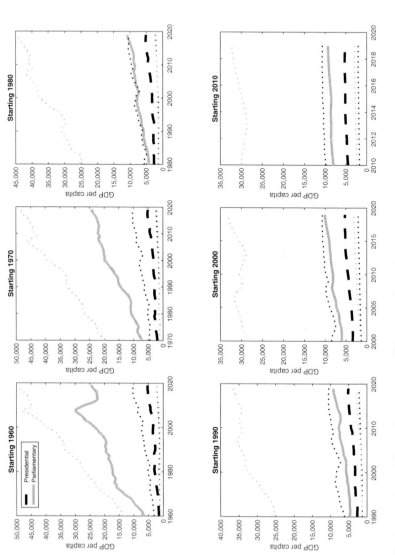

Figure A2.1 GDP per capita and form of government, different starting points.

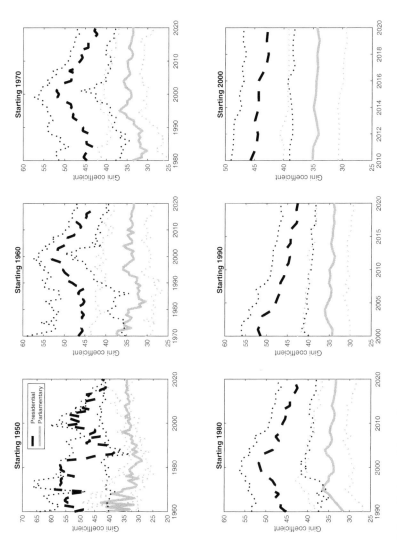

Figure A2.2 Gini coefficient and form of government, different starting points.

List of countries with regime changes according to the Bormann and Golder (2013) dataset, the following countries have had the following changes in their regime:

- Bangladesh: the election of 2008 was recorded as a Civilian dictatorship whereas all other years as a parliamentary democracy.
- Czech Republic: the regime was recorded as semi-presidential democracy after the elections in 2013 whereas before this as a parliamentary democracy.
- France: from 1967, France's regime has been classified as a semi-presidential democracy, before that a parliamentary one.
- Kiribati: since 2012, Kiribati regime has been classified as a presidential democracy, before this a parliamentary one.
- Republic of Korea: since 1988, South Korea has been classified as a presidential democracy; in 1960, they were a parliamentary democracy.
- Sri Lanka: in 1977, Sri Lanka was considered a Civilian dictatorship and before this a parliamentary democracy. Since 1989, Sri Lanka has been classified as a presidential democracy.
- Moldova: in 1998, Moldova was considered a semi-presidential democracy, all other times a parliamentary one.
- Nigeria: in 1964, Nigeria was classified as a parliamentary democracy; in 1979 a presidential democracy; in 1983 a military dictatorship; from 1999 to 2011 a presidential democracy; and since 2015 a semi-presidential democracy.
- Pakistan: in 1977, Pakistan was classified as a military dictatorship and from 1988 a parliamentary democracy.
- Sudan: in 1958, Sudan was considered a military dictatorship and since then a parliamentary democracy.
- Sierra Leone: in 1962, Sierra Leone was classified as a parliamentary democracy; in 1967 a military dictatorship; and from 1996 a presidential democracy.
- Somalia: since 1969, Somalia has been classified as a military dictatorship and before then a parliamentary democracy.
- Suriname: in 1991, Suriname was classified as a presidential democracy, prior to this a parliamentary one.
- Slovak Republic: from 1999 onwards, Slovakia has been classified as a semi-presidential regime, and a parliamentary one prior to this.
- Slovenia: between 2004 and 2011, Slovenia was considered a parliamentary democracy and a semi-presidential one in-between these dates.
- Thailand: in 1976, Thailand was considered a military dictatorship and since 1983 (and prior to 1976) was classified as a parliamentary democracy.

References

Acemoglu, D. (2005) 'Constitutions, politics, and economics: A review essay on Persson and Tabellini's The economic effects of constitutions', *Journal of Economic Literature*, 43, 1025–1048.

Acemoglu, D. (2010) 'Growth and institutions', in *Economic Growth*. London: Palgrave Macmillan, pp. 107–115.

Acemoglu, D. and Johnson, S. (2005) 'Unbundling institutions', *Journal of Political Economy*, 113(5), 949–995.

Acemoglu, D., Johnson, S. and Robinson, J.A. (2001) 'The colonial origins of comparative development: An empirical investigation', *American Economic Review*, 91(5), 1369–1401.

Acemoglu, D., Johnson, S. and Robinson, J.A. (2002) 'Reversal of fortune: Geography and institutions in the making of the modern world income distribution', *The Quarterly Journal of Economics*, 117(4), 1231–1294.

Acemoglu, D. and Robinson, J. (2008) *The Role of Institutions in Growth and Development*. Vol. 10. Washington, DC: World Bank.

Alesina, A. and Perotti, R. (1996) 'Income distribution, political instability, and investment', *European Economic Review*, 40(6), 1203–1228.

Alesina, A. and Summers, L.H. (1993) 'Central bank independence and macroeconomic performance: Some comparative evidence', *Journal of Money, Credit and Banking*, 25(2), 151–162.

Alt, J.E. and Lassen, D.D. (2008) 'Political and judicial checks on corruption: Evidence from American state governments', *Economics & Politics*, 20(1), 33–61.

Anderson, C.J. and Guillory, C.A. (1997) 'Political institutions and satisfaction with democracy: A cross-national analysis of consensus and majoritarian systems', *American Political Science Review*, 91(1), 66–81.

Andrews, J.T. and Montinola, G.R. (2004) 'Veto players and the rule of law in emerging democracies', *Comparative Political Studies*, 37(1), 55–87.

Bagehot, W. (1867) *The English Constitution*. London.

Banerjee, A. and Iyer, L. (2005) 'History, institutions, and economic performance: The legacy of colonial land tenure systems in India', *American Economic Review*, 95(4), 1190–1213.

Bardhan, P. (2005) *Globalization, Inequality, and Poverty: An Overview*. University of California at Berkeley, mimeo.

Barro, R. (1998) *Determinants of Economic Growth: A Cross-Country Empirical Study*. Cambridge, MA and London: The MIT Press.

Barro, R. (2007) 'Democracy and growth', *Journal of Economic Growth*, 1(1) (1996), 1–27.

Barro, R. and Gordon, D.B. (1983) 'Rules, discretion and reputation in a model of monetary policy', *Journal of Monetary Economics*, 12(1), 101–121.

Barro, R. and Lee, J.W. (2013) 'A new data set of educational attainment in the world, 1950–2010', *Journal of Development Economics*, 104, 184–198.

Becker, S.O. and Woessmann, L. (2009) 'Was Weber wrong? A human capital theory of protestant economic history', *The Quarterly Journal of Economics*, 124(2), 531–596.

Bell, D. and Machin, S. (2016) 'Brexit and wage inequality', Technical report, VOX EU.

Bernanke, B.S., Laubach, T., Mishkin, F.S. and Posen, A.S. (1999) *Inflation Targeting*. Princeton: Princeton University Press.

Blume, L., Müller, J., Voigt, S. and Wolf, C. (2009) 'The economic effects of constitutions: Replicating – and extending – Persson and Tabellini', *Public Choice*, 139(1–2), 197–225.

Bordo, M.D. and Meissner, C.M. (2012) 'Does inequality lead to a financial crisis?', *Journal of International Money and Finance*, 31(8), 2147–2161.

Bormann, N.C. (2010) 'Patterns of democracy and its critics', *Living Reviews in Democracy*, 2.

Bormann, N.-C. and Golder, M. (2013) 'Democratic electoral systems around the world, 1946–2011', *Electoral Studies,* 32(2), 360–369.

Buchanan, J.M. and Tullock, G. (1962) *The Calculus of Consent*. Vol. 3. University of Michigan Press. ISBN: 978-0-472-06100-6.

Caliendo, M. and Kopeinig, S. (2008) 'Some practical guidance for the implementation of propensity score matching', *Journal of Economic Surveys*, 22(1), 31–72.

Campos, N.F. and Nugent, J.B. (2002) 'Who is afraid of political instability?', *Journal of Development Economics*, 67(1), 157–172.

Carey, J.M. (2008) 'Presidential versus parliamentary government', in *Handbook of New Institutional Economics*. Berlin, Heidelberg: Springer, pp. 91–122.

Carey, J.M. (2014) 'Presidentialism 25 years after Linz', Keynote address at the Conference on Coalitional Presidentialism at St. Anthony's College, Oxford, on May 2, 2014.

Carney, M. (2015) 'Inflation in a globalised world', Speech at Economic Policy Symposium in Jackson Hole, WY, August 2015.

Cecchetti, S.G. and Krause, S. (2002) 'Central bank structure, policy efficiency, and macroeconomic performance: Exploring empirical relationships', *Review-Federal Reserve Bank of Saint Louis*, 84(4), 47–60.

Cella, M., Iannantuoni, G. and Manzoni, E. (2017) 'Do the right thing: Incentives for policy selection in presidential and parliamentary systems', *Economica*, 84(335), 430–453.

Chandra, S. and Rudra, N. (2015) 'Reassessing the links between regime type and economic performance: Why some authoritarian regimes show stable growth and others do not', *British Journal of Political Science*, 45(2), 253–285.

Cheibub, J.A., Gandhi, J. and Vreeland, J.R. (2010) 'Democracy and dictatorship revisited', *Public Choice*, 143(1–2), 67–101.

Cheibub, J.A., Przeworski, A. and Saiegh, S.M. (2004) 'Government coalitions and legislative success under presidentialism and parliamentarism', *British Journal of Political Science*, 34(4), 565–587.

Ciccarelli, M. and Mojon, B. (2010) 'Global inflation', *The Review of Economics and Statistics*, 92(3), 524–535.

Claessens, S. and Perotti, E. (2007) 'Finance and inequality: Channels and evidence', *Journal of Comparative Economics*, 35(4), 748–773.

Crowe, C. and Meade, E.E. (2008) 'Central bank independence and transparency: Evolution and effectiveness', *European Journal of Political Economy*, 24(4), 763–777.

Cukierman, A., Web, S. and Neyapti, B. (1992) 'Measuring the independence of central banks and its effect on policy outcomes', *World Bank Economic Review*, 6(3), 353–398.

Dehejia, R.H. and Wahba, S. (2002) 'Propensity score-matching methods for non-experimental causal studies', *Review of Economics and Statistics*, 84(1), 51–161.

Easterly, W. and Rebelo, S. (1993) 'Fiscal policy and economic growth', *Journal of Monetary Economics*, 32(3), 417–458.

Eichengreen, B. and Iversen, T. (1999) 'Institutions and economic performance: Evidence from the labour market', *Oxford Review of Economic Policy*, 15(4), 121–138.

Elgie, R. (2005) 'From Linz to Tsebelis: Three waves of presidential/parliamentary studies?, *Democratization*, 12(1), 106–122.

Elgie, R. (2020) 'An Intellectual History of the Concepts of Premier-Presidentialism and President-Parliamentarism', *Political Studies Review*, 18(1), 12–29.

Ellis, A. and Samuels, K. (2009) *Making Presidentialism Work: Sharing and Learning from Global Experience*. Cómo Hacer Que Funcione el Sistema Presidencial (Making Presidentialism Work). México, DF: Universidad Nacional Autónoma de México-Instituto de Investigaciones Jurídicas.

Engvall, J. (2022) 'Between Bandits and Bureaucrats: 30 Years of Parliamentary Development in Kyrgyzstan', Central Asia-Caucasus Institute & Silk Road Studies Program Silk Road Paper, available at www.silkroadstudies.org/publications/silkroad-papers-and-monographs/item/13434-between-bandits-and-bureaucrats-30-years-of-parliamentary-development-in-kyrgyzstan.html

Fish, M.S. and Kroenig, M. (2009) *The Handbook of National Legislatures: A Global Survey*. Cambridge: Cambridge University Press.

Frankel, J.A. and Romer, D.H. (1996) 'Trade and growth: An empirical investigation', NBER Working Paper, No. 5476.

Freedom House (2022) Freedom in the World 2022. https://freedomhouse.org/sites/default/files/2022-02/FIW_2022_PDF_Booklet_Digital_Final_Web.pdf

Galor, O. and Moav, O. (2004) 'From physical to human capital accumulation: Inequality and the process of development', *The Review of Economic Studies*, 71(4), 1001–1026.

Gerring, J. and Thacker, S.C. (2004) 'Political institutions and corruption: The role of unitarism and parliamentarism', *British Journal of Political Science*, 34(2), 295–330.

Gerring, J., Thacker, S.C. and Moreno, C. (2009) 'Are parliamentary systems better?', *Comparative Political Studies*, 42(3), 327–359.

Glaeser, E.L., La Porta, R., Lopez-de-Silanes, F. and Shleifer, A. (2004) 'Do institutions cause growth?', *Journal of Economic Growth*, 9(3), 271–303.

Granovetter, M. (2005) 'The impact of social structure on economic outcomes', *Journal of Economic Perspectives*, 19(1), 33–50.

Gregorini, F. and Longoni, E. (2009) 'Inequality, political systems and public spending', Technical report.

Ha, J., Kose, M.A. and Ohnsorge, F. (eds.) (2019) *Inflation in Emerging and Developing Economies: Evolution, Drivers, and Policies*. Washington, DC: World Bank Publications.

Hall, R.E. and Jones, C.I. (1999) 'Why do some countries produce so much more output per worker than others?', *The Quarterly Journal of Economics*, 114(1), 83–116.

Hansen, C., Hausman, J. and Newey, W. (2008) 'Estimation with many instrumental variables', *Journal of Business & Economic Statistics*, 26(4), 398–422.

Hayo, B. and Voigt, S. (2010) 'Determinants of constitutional change: Why do countries change their form of government?', *Journal of Comparative Economics*, 38(3), 283–305.

Helpman, E. (ed.) (2008) *Institutions and Economic Performance*. Harvard University Press. ISBN: 9780674030770.

Henisz, W.J (2004) 'Political institutions and policy volatility', *Economics & Politics*, 16(1), 1–27.

Hochstetler, K. and Edwards, M.E. (2009) 'Failed presidencies: Identifying and explaining a South American anomaly', *Journal of Politics in Latin America*, 1(2), 31–57.

Kamber, G. and Wong, B. (2020) 'Global factors and trend inflation', *Journal of International Economics*, 122, 103265.

Kedar, O. (2005) 'When moderate voters prefer extreme parties: Policy balancing in parliamentary elections', *American Political Science Review*, 99(2), 185–199.

King, M. (2005) 'What has inflation targeting achieved?', *The Inflation Targeting Debate*, 11–16.

Kirişçi, K. and Toygür, I. (2019) 'Turkey's new presidential system and a changing West: Implications for Turkish foreign policy and Turkey-West relations', Turkey Project Policy Paper, 15.

Knutsen, C.H. (2009) 'The economic growth effect of constitutions revisited', Technical report, Department of Political Science, University of Oslo.

Knutsen, C.H. (2011) 'Which democracies prosper? Electoral rules, form of government and economic growth', *Electoral Studies*, 30(1), 83–90.

Knutsen, C.H. (2021) 'Autocracy and variations in economic development outcomes', in G. Crawford and A.-G. Abdulai (eds.), *Research Handbook on Democracy and Development*. Edward Elgar Publishing. ISSN: 9781788112642.

Knutsen, C.H. and Rasmussen, M.B. (2018) 'Electoral rules, labor market coordination and macroeconomic performance', *Scandinavian Political Studies*, 41(3), 367–378.

Kydland, F. and Prescott, E. (1977) 'Rules rather than discretion: The inconsistency of optimal plans', *Journal of Political Economy*, 85(3), 473–492.

Lijphart, A. (1984) *Democracies: Patterns of Majoritarian & Consensus Government in Twenty-one Countries*. New Haven: Yale University Press.

Lijphart, A. (1994) 'Democracies: Forms, performance, and constitutional engineering', *European Journal of Political Research*, 25(1), 1–17.

Lijphart, A. (2004) 'Constitutional design for divided societies', *Journal of Democracy*, 15(2), 96–109.

Lijphart, A. (2012) *Patterns of Democracy: Government Forms and Performance in Thirty-six Countries*. New Haven: Yale University Press.

Linz, J. (1985) *Presidential or Parliamentary Democracy: Does It Make a Difference?* New Haven: Yale University.

Linz, J. (1990) 'The perils of presidentialism', *Journal of Democracy*, 1(1), 51–69.

Linz, J. (1994) 'Presidential or parliamentary democracy: Does it make a difference?', J.J. Linz and A. Valenzuela (eds.), *The Failure of Presidential Democracy*. Baltimore: John Hopkins University Press.

Mainwaring, S. (1990) 'Presidentialism in Latin America', *Latin American Research Review*, 25(1), 157–179.

Mainwaring, S. (1993) 'Presidentialism, multipartisanism, and democracy the difficult combination', *Comparative Political Studies*, 26(2), 198–228.

Mainwaring, S. and Shugart, M.S. (1997) 'Juan Linz, Presidentialism, and democracy: A critical appraisal', *Comparative Politics*, 29(4), 449–471.

Mauro, P. (1995) 'Corruption and growth', *The Quarterly Journal of Economics*, 110(3), 681–712.

McManus, R. and Ozkan, F.G. (2018) 'Who does better for the economy? Presidents versus parliamentary democracies', *Public Choice*, 176, 361–387.

Milanovic, B. (2018) 'Why inequality matters?', VoxEU, available at https://voxeu.org/content/why-inequality-matters.

Mishkin, F.S. (2001) *From Monetary Targeting to Inflation Targeting (No. 2684)*. Washington, DC: World Bank Publications.

Morgenstern, S., Perez, A. and Peterson, M. (2020) 'Revisiting Shugart and Carey's relation of executive powers and democratic breakdown', *Political Studies Review*, 18(1), 125–144.

Mumtaz, H. and Surico, P. (2012) 'Evolving international inflation dynamics: World and country-specific factors', *Journal of the European Economic Association*, 10(4), 716–734.

Murphy, J. (2020) 'Parliaments and crises: Challenges and innovation', Parliamentary Primer 1, International Institute for Democracy and Electoral Assistance, Stockholm, 2020.

Newey, W.K. (1990) 'Efficient instrumental variables estimation of nonlinear models', *Econometrica*, 809–837.

Nickell, S. and Layard, R. (1999) 'Labor market institutions and economic performance', *Handbook of Labor Economics*, 3, 3029–3084.

Norris, P. (2012) *Making Democratic Governance Work: How Regimes Shape Prosperity, Welfare, and Peace*. Cambridge: Cambridge University Press.

North, D.C. (1993) 'Institutions and economic performance', *Rationality, Institutions and Economic Methodology*, 2, 242–261.

North, D.C. (1990) *Institutions, Institutional Change and Economic Performance*. Cambridge: Cambridge University Press.

North, D.C. (2005a) *Understanding the Process of Economic Change*. Princeton: Princeton University Press.

North, D.C. (2005b) 'Institutions and the performance of economics over time', in C. Ménard and M.M. Shirley (eds.), *Handbook of New Institutional Economics*. Dordrecht: Springer, pp. 21–30.

OECD (2015) *In It Together: Why Less Inequality Benefits All*. Paris: OECD Publishing.

Panizza, U. (2002) 'Income inequality and economic growth: Evidence from American data', *Journal of Economic Growth*, 7(1), 25–41.

Persson, T. (2005) 'Forms of democracy, policy and economic development', Technical report, National Bureau of Economic Research.

Persson, T., Roland, G. and Tabellini, G. (2000) 'Comparative politics and public finance', *Journal of Political Economy*, 108(6), 1121–1161.

Persson, T. and Tabellini, G. (2003) *The Economic Effects of Constitutions*. Cambridge, MA: The MIT Press.

Piketty, T. (2003) 'Income inequality in France, 1901–1998', *Journal of Political Economy*, 111(5), 1004–1042.

Piketty, T. and Saez, E. (2003) 'Income inequality in the United States, 1913–1998', *The Quarterly Journal of Economics*, 118(1), 1–41.

Polillo, S. and Guillén, M.F. (2005) 'Globalization pressures and the state: The worldwide spread of central bank independence', *American Journal of Sociology*, 110(6), 1764–1802.

Price, D.K. (1943) 'The Parliamentary and Presidential Systems', *Public Administration Review*, 3(4), 317–334.

Rajan, R. (2010) 'How inequality fueled the crisis', *Project Syndicate*, 9.

Reynal-Querol, M. and Montalvo, J.G. (2005) 'Ethnic polarization, potential conflict and civil war', *American Economic Review*, 95(3), 796–816.

Riggs, F.W. (1988) 'The survival of presidentialism in America: Para-constitutional practices', *International Political Science Review*, 9(4), 247–278.

Riggs, F.W. (1993) 'Fragility of the third world's regimes', *International Social Science Journal*, 45(2), 199–243.

Rockey, J. (2012) 'Reconsidering the fiscal effects of constitutions', *European Journal of Political Economy*, 28(3), 313–323.

Rodrik, D. (2000) 'Institutions for high-quality growth: What they are and how to acquire them', *Studies in Comparative International Development*, 35(3), 3–31.

Rodrik, D. (2004) 'Institutions and economic performance-getting institutions right', *CESIfo DICE Report*, 2(2), 10–15.

Rodrik, D., Subramanian, A. and Trebbi, F. (2004) 'Institutions rule: The primacy of institutions over geography and integration in economic development', *Journal of Economic Growth*, 9(2), 131–165.

Rogoff, M.A. (2011) *French Constitutional Law: Cases and Materials*. Carolina Academic Press. ISBN: 1594606544.

Rogoff, K. (1985) 'The optimal degree of commitment to an intermediate monetary target', *The quarterly journal of economics, 100*(4), 1169–1189.

Roper, S.D. (2008) 'From semi-presidentialism to parliamentarism: Regime change and presidential power in Moldova', *Europe-Asia Studies*, 60(1), 113–126.

Sargan, J.D. (1958) 'The estimation of economic relationships using instrumental variables', *Econometrica*, 393–415.

Scarrow, H.A. (1974) 'Parliamentary and presidential government compared', *Current History*, 66(394), 264–267.

Scully, G.W. (1988) 'The institutional framework and economic development', *Journal of Political Economy*, 96(3), 652–662.

Sedelius, T. and Linde, J. (2018) 'Unravelling semi-presidentialism: Democracy and government performance in four distinct regime types', *Democratization*, 25(1), 136–157.

Shleifer, A. and Vishny, R.W. (1994) 'Politicians and firms', *The Quarterly Journal of Economics*, 109(4), 995–1025.

Shugart, M.S. (1999) 'Presidentialism, parliamentarism, and the provision of collective goods in less-developed countries', *Constitutional Political Economy*, 10(1), 53–88.

Shugart, M.S. and Carey, J. (1992) *Presidents and Assemblies: Constitutional Design and Electoral Dynamics*. Cambridge: Cambridge University Press.

Somer, M. (2019) 'Turkey: The slippery slope from reformist to revolutionary polarization and democratic breakdown', *The ANNALS of the American Academy of Political and Social Science*, 681(1), 42–61.

Sovey, A.J. and Green, D.P. (2011) 'Instrumental variables estimation in political science: A readers' guide', *American Journal of Political Science*, 55(1), 188–200.

Staiger, D. and Stock, J.H. (1997) 'Instrumental variables regression with weak instruments', *Econometrica*, 65(3), 557–586.

Stepan, A. and Skach, C. (1993) 'Constitutional frameworks and democratic consolidation: Parliamentarianism versus presidentialism', *World Politics*, 46(1), 1–22.

Stiglitz, J.E. (2012) 'Macroeconomic fluctuations, inequality, and human development', *Journal of Human Development and Capabilities*, 13(1), 31–58.

Stock, J.H., Wright, J.H. and Yogo, M. (2002) 'A survey of weak instruments and weak identification in generalized method of moments', *Journal of Business & Economic Statistics*, 20(4), 518–529.

Svensson, L.E. (2010) 'Inflation targeting', in *Handbook of Monetary Economics*. Vol. 3. Elsevier, pp. 1237–1302.

Tabellini, G. (2008) 'Institutions and culture', *Journal of the European Economic Association*, 6(2–3), 255–294.

Thoemmes, F.J. and Kim, E.S. (2011) 'A systematic review of propensity score methods in the social sciences', *Multivariate Behavioral Research*, 46(1), 90–118.

Tsebelis, G. (1995) 'Decision making in political systems: Veto players in presidentialism, parliamentarism, multicameralism and multipartyism', *British Journal of Political Science*, 25(3), 289–325.

Uberti, L.J. and Knutsen, C.H. (2021) 'Institutions, human capital and economic growth', in E. Douarin and O. Havrylyshyn (eds.), *The Palgrave Handbook of Comparative Economics*. Palgrave Macmillan. ISBN: 978-3-030-50887-6.

Van Treeck, T. (2014) 'Did inequality cause the US financial crisis?', *Journal of Economic Surveys*, 28(3), 421–448.

Wilson, W. (1885) *Congressional Government*. New York: Houghton Mifflin.

Index

Note: Page numbers in *italics* indicate a figure and page numbers in **bold** indicate a table on the corresponding page.

Printed in the United States
by Baker & Taylor Publisher Services